PROPHETIC COUNTER INSURGENCE

Book 6 – The Prophetic Field Guide Series

Second Edition

COLETTE TOACH

AMI BOOKSHOP

www.ami-bookshop.com

PROPHETIC COUNTER INSURGENCE
Book 6 – The Prophetic Field Guide Series
Second Edition

ISBN-10: 1626641048
ISBN-13: 978-1-62664-104-4

Copyright © 2016 by Apostolic Movement International, LLC
All rights reserved
5663 Balboa Ave #416,
San Diego,
California 92111,
United States of America

1st Printing December 2015
2nd Edition May 2016

Published by Apostolic Movement International, LLC
E-mail Address: admin@ami-bookshop.com
Web Address: www.ami-bookshop.com

All rights reserved under International Copyright Law.
Contents may not be reproduced in whole or in part in any form without the express written consent of the publisher.

Unless specified, all Scripture references taken from the New King James Version®. Copyright © 1982 by Thomas Nelson. Used by permission. All rights reserved.

CONTENTS

STRATEGIES IN SPIRITUAL WARFARE

CHAPTER 01 – STRATEGIES IN SPIRITUAL WARFARE

History is written by the victors. Our story is being unfolded before our eyes and in a hundred years from now, what will the story of the Church be? What will be written of the prophets upon the walls, and those who travailed in the thick of battle?

What will be said of the apostles who built cities? What of the evangelists who were found in the trenches fighting tooth and nail for each and every soul that made their way into the Kingdom of God?

Today, you have the unique opportunity to make history. From your prayer closet, out in the field, or the time you reached out and saved a single sheep from "slipping over the edge."

Victories are found in the most unique places and the greatest wars won were not always those fought with strict battle lines. In fact, it reminds me of a history event I learned in school.

Growing up in South Africa, we were taught about the various wars that shaped the nation. One event was called "The Boer War." The Boers were the first settlers trying hard to stay their ground.

The opposing force? The British. I am not a historian, so I will spare you dates and specifics, and draw your attention to the interesting part of this encounter.

You see in that time, warfare was done in a specific way. The British would don their bright red coats, and stand on battle lines with weapons drawn. Then in a very organized manner, engage the enemy in harmonious step.

I can imagine it looked impressive. The Boers were impressed too – impressed by how easily that line could be scattered. They did not have bright red coats. They did not have fancy weapons. So they did the next best thing… they changed the battlefield.

While the British were breaking for afternoon tea, or waiting to get into line, the Boers decided that the "line up" was not their style. They said to themselves, "We are not going to get them on the field, instead we will get them somewhere on the way. We can wait for their tea time and then attack them."

They took all the weaknesses of this big British army and they engaged in Counter Insurgence warfare.

Instead of meeting the British on the field, as was customary, they did everything differently. They realized that one of the main weaknesses of the British was that they did everything so orderly and so expected their enemy to respond in like fashion.

The Boers said, "Forget it. We are not going to do it your way. We are going to do it our way."

They snuck into the British camps and attacked them in the night. They attacked them on the road. They hid amongst the rocks and they blended in with their surroundings.

For a long time, this sent the British running until they got wiser and thought, "We better change our tactics."

In *Prophetic Warrior*, I taught you about your enemy. You are well aware of what he looks like, and how he likes to engage in battle. Now it is time to change the battlefield and engage him in a way that he does not expect.

KEY PRINCIPLE

> When you know your enemy, you know his weaknesses. When you know his weaknesses, you can take him out easily.

The enemy is just like the bright red army, with their flashy coats and muskets gleaming in the sun. You can see him coming from a mile, if you know what to look for.

You have had your fair share of tackling spirits of infirmity and fear. In fact, by now taking down power and ruler demons should be second nature to you.

In this chapter I want to take you even deeper into spiritual warfare. Firstly, we are going to take a closer look at the princes of the air that control it all. Then we are going to look at how exactly the prophet is called to take them down using the strategy of counter insurgence.

CHANGE OF FOCUS

For the longest time the Lord had me doing spiritual warfare at the lower levels – winning one battle at a time. It was during this time that I came to understand and see the structure of satan's kingdom. After some time though, the Lord told me to change tactics.

He told me that instead of focusing on just one problem at a time, I had to aim higher. Instead of tackling a single financial need or just one attack, to look beyond that. To rather stand in faith for favor and prosperity.

Instead of taking on one demon at a time, to go right to the top.

> *Acts 5:36 For some time ago Theudas rose up, claiming to be somebody. A number of men, about four hundred, joined him. He was slain, and all who obeyed him were scattered and came to nothing.*
> *37 After this man, Judas of Galilee rose up in the days of the census, and drew away many people after him. He also perished, and all who obeyed him were dispersed.*

Gamaliel gave some good counsel here when speaking of the Disciples. He shared how leaders had come before them and when those leaders fell… everyone that followed them scattered. Well I am sure he did not know at the time that the One who lead the Disciples had not only died already, but had resurrected!

GO TO THE TOP

The principle remains the same though. Strike the leader and their followers will scatter. Tired of engaging in hours of spiritual warfare? Then go to the top! Stop fussing about with the little principality demons and go to the princes of the air that structured their straight battle lines.

So what do these princes look like exactly? Well that is what I am about to share with you. I have selected the ones that I have faced a lot in my spiritual encounters. You are about to see how much you have also come against them at one time or another. They are the big shots that control the various systems of the world.

It is time to expose them for who they are to remind them who is really in charge. We serve a King that is undefeated. We serve the Prince of Peace that cannot be shaken and a Spirit of power that is armed to the teeth. I would say that the odds are in our favor – wouldn't you?

THE COUNCIL OF WICKEDNESS

Because I am covering various princes, when I speak of them collectively, I am going to refer to them as the Council of Wickedness. I do not doubt that as I work through this list that others might come to your mind also.

There is one point to note though. Regardless of how strong these princes seem or how overwhelming the systems of the world are, the greater power is on our side. We never need to be afraid or feel defeated. Quite the opposite in fact. We can rest in faith, hope, and love, knowing that this battle has already been won. We just need to stand on that victory!

APOLLYON – MEDICAL SYSTEM

> *Revelation 9:7 The shape of the locusts was like horses prepared for battle. On their heads were crowns of something like gold, and their faces were like the faces of men.*
> *8 They had hair like women's hair, and their teeth were like lions' teeth.*
> *9 And they had breastplates like breastplates of iron, and the sound of their wings was like the sound of chariots with many horses running into battle.*
> *10 They had tails like scorpions, and there were stings in their tails. Their power was to hurt men five months.*
> *11 And they had as king over them the angel of the bottomless pit, whose name in Hebrew is Abaddon, but in Greek he has the name Apollyon.*

Apollyon. He is the prince over the medical systems and the one who organizes the physical attacks that you face time and again. There is nothing that tries your faith more than pain.

After spending days in pain, your good resolve is eaten away. It makes you weary and steals your sound mind. Is it no wonder then that satan uses sickness more than anything to cripple the Church?

With every revival that has come upon the Church, what has been the emphasis? Healing! Why? It is because each time that the Holy Spirit wanted to manifest His power, He did so by setting his people free from the clutches of Apollyon!

He is the serpent who continues to "strike the heel" of God's creation – hating the fact that we have authority in this earth! We are everything the enemy cannot stand – God's own sons and daughters. We hold the place that he wanted and we have the authority he craved. Our very faith is an insult to him.

What better way to steal that authority and faith, than by bringing about physical attack? How easy it is to write that attack off as "physical or mental illness"? We call it "vitamin deficiencies" and "genetics." How about we label it correctly? Let's just call it what it is – demonic attack!

The work of Apollyon in this earth is to discredit and destroy God's beautiful creation. Our God is not the author of sickness and disease. Want proof of that? Just follow the ministry of Jesus. He could not even sit down for lunch without stretching out His hand to heal in compassion.

How sickness came about because of sin and bondage is a message for another book. (You can listen to the *Tree of Life* message if you want more on that)

For now, I want you to look beyond your physical attack right now and realize, that once again, you wrestle not with flesh and blood. You wrestle with wickedness in high places and it is high time that they are dethroned!

ATTACK OF THE MIND

A physical attack creates the perfect environment for the battlefield of your soul to come into play. You wake up in the middle of the night with a throbbing pain in your tooth and before you can get a handle on it, you think, "Is that an abscess?"

Your blood pressure goes up and before you can say, "generational curse" your mind is filled with words like, "You are going to be just like your father who died of a heart attack..."

Fear! You begin to grasp at straws and while those physical symptoms remain, the thoughts that are added to them try and convince you of the "truth" that satan wants to indoctrinate you with.

Do you know when the best time is to fight cancer, high blood pressure, diabetes, obesity and every other sickness? It is in the moment that Apollyon sets his sights on you and puts his hordes of scorpions to attack.

In the passage above, Apollyon leads an army of locusts with tails of scorpions. Impressive... except for the fact that this passage blows all of that out of the water:

> *Luke 10:19 Behold, I give you the authority to trample on serpents and scorpions, and over all the power of the enemy, and nothing shall by any means hurt you.*
> *20 Nevertheless do not rejoice in this, that the spirits are subject to you, but rather rejoice because your names are written in heaven.*

If you entertain that first symptom and accompanying thoughts, satan has you right where he wants you. He will have you bound up in the battlefield in your soul, and the fear you find there, will paralyze you. That is the work of Apollyon. It is warfare.

You need to nip it in the bud. When those thoughts first start to come into your mind, you need to stop and say, "That thought is not based on the Word."

That is why I challenged you to get into the Word so many times through each book in this series. When the Word is your foundation, and thoughts that are contrary to the Word are coming to your mind, you will say, "No. The Word says that God has not given us a spirit of fear, but of power, love, and a sound mind."

Entertain fear, and guilt is right around the corner. You begin saying to yourself, "I should have had that checked. I should not have eaten that junk food. I should have obeyed my spirit…"

Yes, Apollyon's work here is done. You can be left quite easily in the hands of the power and ruler demons to finish you off now. Before you know it, you are in a battle that consumes your time and energy.

You are going from one doctor to the other and are spending hours on the internet trying to find a solution. The more you look, the worse it sounds. From one webpage to the other, your worse fears are realized – there is no doubt about it – that bright pimple on your nose that erupted overnight can only mean one thing – YOU ARE GOING TO DIE!

Does that sound melodramatic? If so, then you have clearly not been near someone who is under serious attack from Apollyon.

> **KEY PRINCIPLE**
>
> Just like when we walk in faith, we walk from hope to hope – when you walk in fear, you walk from despair to despair.

Stop it! Turn off the TV and computer. Stop going from doctor to doctor and take a moment to clear your head. Satan has you fighting a battle that he has perfected ever since the Garden of Eden. Do you think you have what it takes to defeat his fear with your own?

No, time for some counter insurgence! Time to change things up.

I know the Word and the Word is clear. You do not have to take those thoughts. You can cast down those imaginations. Bring your thoughts captive and bring them in line with the Word of God.

If you feel that you need to repent, do it. It takes two minutes. I have taken you through this already. "Father, forgive me. Apollyon, get lost!"

The great thing about the attacks on your mind is that they are easy to overcome... once you open your mouth and say something!

GEAR UP!

However, if you are focusing on one little spirit of infirmity after the other, you are going to be wasting your time and energy for a long time. Sometimes you will have a spirit of infirmity attack you and so you can shake it off.

However, when you continually have physical attacks and disfavor in the medical systems of the world – gear up! Apollyon is up to his tricks again! Forget about fighting the little headache and stubbed toe.

Forget messing with all the little spirits of infirmity and head straight to the big boss. Once he is bound, then the rest need to follow suit.

This attack is very common to those who rise up in the Kingdom of God. When I think back on so many of God's generals, I see how satan destroyed them with physical attack. He continued until he won and snuffed another light in the darkness.

You no longer need to be the one with satan's crosshairs pointed to your head. You do not need to suffer. You do not need to take these physical distractions – because that is exactly what they are – distractions! They keep leading you astray and running after them, instead of building the Kingdom of God!

Instead of ministering and building the work, this attack causes you to spend all your faith, finances and thoughts on your physical condition. Time to get the helmet of salvation on again. Get a new view and shake off this attack. Bind Apollyon and when you do, something miraculous will happen.

VICTORY THROUGH MIRACULOUS HEALING

I have seen the Lord do amazing things in this very realm of spiritual warfare. For many years I suffered with terrible arthritis. It was a generational curse that satan used against my family members, to slow them down from doing the work of God.

I was pregnant with my fourth child and in terrible pain. We had tried everything from massage to chiropractic care and medications. We prayed and stood in faith, but there came a defining moment one day as I went downstairs to do laundry.

I had tried to pull my wet laundry from the washer to put it into the dryer, and all the muscles in my back seized up. I could not move. Something in me just snapped. That was really enough! I had enough of the pain. I had enough of the attack. In that moment I got a rhema, "I do not need to take this."

A strong conviction rose from within me and I bound the prince and all the hordes of hell that had come against me. It was as if a switch went off and every muscle released in my back. The pain left immediately and my joints eased. I completed my load of laundry and skipped back upstairs.

My muscles ached a little the next few days as they healed naturally from there. Day by day I became stronger and I have not suffered from arthritis ever again.

Victory Through Medical System

Now Craig had a different problem. He was terribly near sighted. For years he trusted God to heal his eyes. As we progressed and rose up in ministry though, this prayer was left on the backburner, as we gave our focus to the work of the ministry.

Glasses and his eyesight started becoming quite an annoyance with all our traveling and flying here and there. It was our anniversary and we had some time together and decided to go swimming in the ocean. A huge wave decided to take ownership of his glasses, making him frustrated.

When we got home, I felt led in my spirit to look online for some solutions. The Lord led me to a doctor in Mexico who was performing an amazing procedure that would give Craig 20/20 vision.

The Holy Spirit told me, "Make the initial appointment to get him tested for compatibility." Talk about favor! Not only could they see us right away, but the procedure was done on the same day of the appointment. He went into the appointment with glasses and left later in the afternoon without them.

Now you must know that I was brought up in the Pentecostal era. All of my family was literally born into the turn of the century revivals of God. Going to the doctor was akin to seeing the devil. I was conflicted. The Lord helped set me straight though when I asked Him about it. He said to me,

"Colette I know that you have the faith to believe for Craig's eyesight, but right now I need you focused on the ministry… not your personal needs. So I have arranged for it to be taken care of in the way I deem. Will you allow me to heal you in the way I choose, or will you try to dictate to me how I should heal?"

Not only did the Lord provide the finances for the procedure miraculously, but He also arranged for favor and the perfect person to do the job. I witnessed what it looked like when the Lord is put in charge of the medical system. It can be turned to our favor, if only our faith is in the Lord, and not in ourselves!

You cannot get this kind of victory though if you are so bound by fear and pain that you cannot think straight. So deal with Apollyon first. Bind the fear and bring your body into line with the truth of the Word. From there, the Lord can give you revelation on the next step to take.

That is the great thing about being a prophet. The Lord can show you exactly where this attack is coming from. He can tell you exactly who is calling the shots, so that you know where to aim your blood-stained arrows.

PHARAOH – FINANCIAL SYSTEM

> *Ezekiel 31:17 They also went down to hell with it, with those slain by the sword; and those who were its strong arm dwelt in its shadows among the nations.*
> *18 'To which of the trees in Eden will you then be likened in glory and greatness? Yet you shall be brought down with the trees of Eden to the depths of the earth; you shall lie in the midst of the uncircumcised, with those slain by the sword. This is Pharaoh and all his multitude,' says the Lord God.*

You end up accidentally not stopping at a stop sign and then you get a ticket in the mail.

You file your taxes, and it turns out that you did not pay enough, meaning that your savings just got eaten up. Then, there is the health insurance that you thought you were up to date on, but then they come knocking for their pound of flesh.

Hello Pharaoh. Any attack that you start experiencing from the world system is coming from Pharaoh.

You are definitely going to face this in ministry. The world is not happy to just let you rise up and stand in the light. Pharaoh is not going to just let you come in and take his money. So you will find that these attacks come when you start believing God for finances.

When you start having pressure from the financial systems of the world, this is Pharaoh coming at you and he is one of the most obvious. Well, once you identify his tricks, it is obvious. What trips you up every time though, is that it takes a couple of bouts of parrying a theft and blocking a destruction before you get it.

You usually realize that you are under attack when your bank account goes into overdraft or find out that someone stole your ATM card and went on a spending spree with it!

Once you have Pharaoh's number, his work is quite obvious because he attacks by using theft and destruction.

When this happens, stop screaming and yelling at your lawyer and at the government and complaining about how bad things are. Stop writing nasty letters and posting on forums about how much your government needs to change.

Maybe it helps you to let off some steam, but it does not solve your problem. The attacks that you are facing, are coming from a higher power than your government.

These attacks are coming from Pharaoh. If you want to survive in this world, and certainly in ministry, you have to rise up and start coming against Pharaoh.

You are not wrestling with the government or the law. You are wrestling with Pharaoh – the prince in charge of the financial systems.

KEY PRINCIPLE

> If you want to see a victory in your life, you need to get on your knees, pick up your sword, and fight the enemy in the only language that he understands. You fight him with the sword of the Lord, the blood of Christ, and the word of your testimony.

That is how you are going to overcome him. Once you identify this attack in your life, the enemy's days are numbered.

For the most part, once you get this conviction most people identify the attacks of Pharaoh when he starts stealing finances.

STONES TO BREAD

However, the problem is that most people try to fix it by using the arm of the flesh instead of the might of the Spirit.

You say, "Let's get a bunch of people together and get a vote going." You leave out the most important phase of warfare, which is the sword of the Spirit. You need to pick it up and say, "Pharaoh, let God's people go. Let me go. Let my finances go. How dare you mess with me? You loose them right now in the name of Jesus."

Don't you get it? All you are doing is turning stones to bread. Now tell me, when satan tempted Jesus to turn those stones to bread, why didn't Jesus do it?

> *Matthew 4:3 Now when the tempter came to Him, he said, If You are the Son of God, command that these stones become bread.*
> *4 But He answered and said, It is written, Man shall not live by bread alone, but by every word that proceeds from the mouth of God.*

Jesus could easily do it – He was the son of God. He had not eaten and bread was not forbidden. So why did he decline? Do you see it? Sure enough, Jesus could do it, but he refused to use his power to feed himself. He refused to do it in his own strength, but decided to allow God to provide instead!

KEY PRINCIPLE

Every time you try and fight Pharaoh with your flesh, you are turning stones to bread.

When Jesus walked this earth, He called tax collectors to His arms and drank wine with Pharisees. He did not struggle with the people in charge of making the laws. He sure made them responsible for their sin, but His warfare was done half naked, nailed to a tree.

When all was said and done, the Father sent angels to minister to Him. Jesus fought the prince of darkness with blood and overcame.

The demons inspiring man to come against you are just servants. Curses of poverty, theft and destruction? They are just tools in Pharaoh's hand.

Want to get the house of satan to come into line with the Word of God? Stop ordering around the servants. Instead go straight to the man in charge and say, "Sort your servants out." There is power in doing warfare at that level.

By now, I have taken away the fear of doing warfare. When you stand in the knowledge of the Word and you stand in the power of the blood, nothing can stand before you.

This is a topic close to my heart because of the personal and ministry struggles we have had with finances. Next to sickness, it is the one attack that satan will use time and again to destroy ministries.

He will use the banking systems to make changes so that churches lose property. He will steal the blessings that God does give, and cause holes to form in your moneybags. Sure, he has been given license (as we discussed in *Prophetic Warrior*) but that does not mean we just leave him to it!

Yes, close those open doors. Remove his license – but do not leave it there! Once you have taken away his license you must now take your land back.

This is the mistake I see so often with many. They err on one side or the other. The first side is that they think it is all about binding demons.

You bind Pharaoh again and again, and manage to squeeze a bit of finances out of him. All the while your back door is wide open to the thief! Close the door. Then give Pharaoh a bloody nose.

Then the second mistake: You are so busy closing the back door, you do not go the next step forward to take back what he stole!

> *Proverbs 6:30 People do not despise a thief If he steals to satisfy himself when he is starving. 31 Yet when he is found, he must restore sevenfold; He may have to give up all the substance of his house.*

Once you have found satan stealing from you, stand on his neck, because he can give it back sevenfold! Sometimes we are just so happy that we found the open door that satan has been using for so many years, that we forget to take back what he stole!

What has Pharaoh stolen from you? Has he been destroying your ministry and family by eating up every blessing that God has given to you? Has his black hand been strangling every source of provision?

This is not God's perfect will. You need finances to do this work – so do not sit down and take it.

VICTORY THROUGH THE FINANCIAL SYSTEMS

Because of the ministry families we support internationally, finances are a big issue for us. When Craig and I lack… it is not our bare table that bothers us. It is the thought of each family not having food to put before their children. This is something very close to our hearts, and is one thing we bring up in prayer a lot.

To illustrate what victory looks like in this area, I am reminded of a vision the Lord gave me at the beginning of 2014. I was in prayer for the year ahead and asking the Lord for the next step for our ministry.

Suddenly I felt as if I was lifted up and saw myself standing in a huge throne room. It was not the Lord's Throne Room though – this one belonged to Pharaoh. It was as if I was standing there just watching the goings-on.

He sat on a huge throne with servants running here and there. His throne was lifted up by all the banks of the world as if each one was a brick on which he rested. His footstool was the resources that the world had to offer.

Larger than life and arrogant, he was dressed like Pharaoh of old – the god of this world. The Lord had me look closer and took me down a level to view what was going on under his throne.

There I saw many passageways and treasure rooms filled to the brim with the wealth of the wicked. Pharaoh used it as he pleased to further his own desires. It was so big, that I felt a bit intimidated at first.

The Lord said to me, "But look closer Colette." It was then, that I saw something amazing. I saw that there was a tiny hole in the wall of each of these treasure rooms, allowing just enough finances to escape and flow into another room – one positioned exactly under Pharaoh.

The Lord said to me, "Do you see that wealth accumulating in the room there? It is a room that Pharaoh does not see. This room is for you and I am going to cause you to steal from satan, from right under his nose. You do not need to be afraid of the kingdoms of the world, because they are here to serve my good will!"

It was not very long after that we experienced our first miracle that lined up with this vision. One of my spiritual kids shared that there was a fund at his work that allowed him to use an accumulated amount of finances towards any form of education of his choice.

He said that if we could present a training regime with materials for him, he could present it to his workplace and they would fund it. We did so and the ministry gained $10,000! Money was taken directly out of satan's treasure house. The miraculous part was that just after we received the finances, the company in question stopped giving this concession. Perfect timing – all under God's control.

Pharaoh might look "larger than life" when you stand in front of him, but never forget that the Lord drowned him, and all his hordes, with just one breath of his mouth.

PERSIA – POLITICAL SYSTEM

> *Daniel 10:12 Then he said to me, "Do not fear, Daniel, for from the first day that you set your heart to understand, and to humble yourself before your God, your words were heard; and I have come because of your words.*
> *13 But the prince of the kingdom of Persia withstood me twenty- one days; and behold, Michael, one of the chief princes, came to help me, for I had been left alone there with the kings of Persia.*

> *Daniel 6:8 Now, O king, establish the decree and sign the writing, so that it cannot be changed, according to the law of the Medes and Persians, which does not alter.*

With technology, borders are getting closer and closer. As ministers, visas and travel paperwork are part of our daily lives. I gave birth to two of my daughters in South Africa, another daughter in Mexico, and my son in the United States. Have you ever been "outside the box?"

If you want to feel the pressure of the prince of Persia, then just try to travel the world to do the work of God. If he cannot discourage you through sickness or financial lack, he will use politics to destroy you.

I experienced this attack firsthand many times. Laws that are put in place to try and restrict the reach of the church. Governments that outlaw Christianity with one signature and promote abortion with another.

Having traveled a lot and also interacted with people from every nation, allow me to break your limited thinking a little bit. Your country is not the only one with bad laws! Your government is not the only one who likes to line their pockets and control the passes.

Welcome to the prince of Persia's stomping ground. There is good news though. Just as Esther and Mordecai could use the law of the Medes and Persians against them... we can do the same.

Why do you keep fighting the systems of this world? Have you learned nothing yet? Just put another prince in their place. Give the Prince of Peace some license here and watch God take what satan sought for evil, and turn it around for our good!

When you find yourself bound up with newly passed laws that restrict you, do not be afraid. Esther's knees went weak when she heard from Mordecai that the king had decreed the death of every Jew.

She never asked to be Queen. She had not asked to stand in the middle of a raging war without and political alliances within. Yet when God's people needed it most, a savior was found bathed in perfume and draped in silk. She did not take a sword to the throne room of the king. She took the Spirit of God and found favor in the sight of both God and man.

> *KEY PRINCIPLE*
>
> Do you know what the ultimate warfare is against the prince of Persia? It is not a sword – it is the shield of faith, carried with favor. Stop praying for changes in the laws and start praying for favor!

Begin praying that the Lord will put the right people in the right places. Start praying that every law made will benefit the Kingdom of God! You do not realize the power you have in your mouth prophet of God. I have seen the Lord change entire laws on our behalf.

VICTORY IN POLITICS

For many years we lived in Mexico under an extended visitor's visa. It was a hassle and costly to renew every year. We had been giving our visa situation to the Lord. We needed something more stable that gave us the ability to move around easier.

At the end of 2013 a reform took place in the Mexican government and along with that dramatic changes in their immigration laws. For many the changes were destructive and there were some that lost their immigration status.

We were not concerned when we went to the office at the end of the year to renew our paperwork. Whatever was going to happen, was in God's hand. We did not expect what happened next.

The official took our paperwork and said, "No. This is the wrong form. You must fill out another one." We filled them in and handed in some other forms that they asked for.

A couple of weeks later we came to pick up our papers and could only stand in awe as we saw what God had done. Craig and I were speechless… they had awarded us permanent residence status.

With all the changes, the office was trying to process everyone quickly so that they could all be on board with the changes for the new year. Our paperwork renewal had come up at just the right time for them to give us favor and issue us with a status that would ordinarily taken a few more years (and a lot more paperwork) to attain. Now that's God.

That is what it looks like when the prince of Persia thinks he is "all that" and the Lord reminds him exactly who is in charge!

We get so caught up in the magnitude of the systems of the world that we easily take our eyes off the throne room that is suspended above the earth, moon, sun and planets... that of our mighty God!

Isn't this the kind of favor that Daniel had? It is the kind of favor we can have as well, if we just stand on what God has given to us.

TYRE – COMMERCIAL SYSTEMS: THE MARKETPLACE

> *1 Kings 5:1 Now Hiram king of Tyre sent his servants to Solomon, because he heard that they had anointed him king in place of his father, for Hiram had always loved David.*

Just try to start a business and watch the prince of Tyre get on your case. He will tie you up with paperwork and redirect contracts to your competitors. You will see this especially if you want to use any of those finances for the work of God.

We make the same mistake with the prince of Tyre as we often do with Pharaoh. Instead of putting your efforts into the spiritual realm, you try to block his attack with "better business practice."

Yes, good business practices will make people like you. Principles like that will open doors for you. What happens though when you have done all you can and your balance sheet still looks like the battle of blood river?

Succeeding in the marketplace as a Christian is going to take a lot more than just good business practice. It is going to take a lot more than a couple of "self-help" seminars to make you succeed.

So after you have programmed your mind with the latest "big marketing" technique and spent thousands learning from the "gurus," perhaps you will be ready for the most important truth of all.

> *Deuteronomy 8:17 Then you say in your heart, My power and the might of my hand have gained me this wealth.*
> *18 "And you shall remember the Lord your God, for it is He who gives you power to get wealth, that He may establish His covenant which He swore to your fathers, as it is this day*

KEY PRINCIPLE

Just like favor is the shield you war against the prince of Persia with, the wisdom of God is the ultimate atom bomb against the prince of Tyre and his cronies.

Solomon understood the power of this, and it was through the wisdom God gave to him that he used the king of Tyre to his own ends. Tired of feeling the wall of

the commercial system pushed up against your face?
Then change battlefields.

Stop trying to play at satan's game. When will you
learn? Did Solomon travel to the Queen of Sheba to
gain her wisdom for his kingdom? No, the nations
came to him. When the Church starts realizing that it is
through the wisdom of God that we will shine, it will
throw off the filthy rags of the systems of the world.

Your business, workplace, and job should be a source
of blessing to the church and your family. Feeling
squeezed? The prince of Persia is turning up the heat.
He enjoys using this system to influence the church,
and control it from within.

He loves it when he can use a worldly boss to steal
your faith, hope, and love. Nothing delights him more
than to make you feel inferior and look down his nose
at you. He likes to trick you into believing that you do
not have what it takes.

He will parade his great accomplishments before you
and do to you like Hiram did to Solomon. He will look
at the cities that you have, and look down his nose at
them. He will deem them unworthy as if you are not
worth his efforts.

Turn the tables on him! Do you know what Solomon
did with the cities that Hiram turned his nose up at? He
built them up and gave a place for the children of Israel
to live. When God gives you a vision to rise up in the
marketplace, you have been gifted with no small task.

The prince of Tyre will raise up everyone around you to oppose your ideas. They will look down their nose at you and scoff at your attempts. The business world will press against you and try to push you down.

In these times, you do not need to fight man against man. It is spiritual warfare and you need to see that your greatest weapon here is wisdom! Wisdom to circumvent the systems of this world and authority to bind the prince of Tyre!

Not only does the Lord want you to do spiritual warfare, but to get to the place where what satan used to pressure you, can thrust you forward! In the end Solomon used the strengths of Tyre to build the Temple and his own house!

VICTORY OVER TYRE

Do I know this prince demon? You cannot try to do any kind of business in any country without coming into loggerheads with him! This became our reality as the Lord started leading us to produce materials and sell books to support the work of God.

You would not believe the challenges you will face living in one country and trying to collect finances from another. Business registrations, bank accounts and paperwork allowing you to do trade. Craig and I did not have business training.

Craig studied at a trade school and is handy with a power drill, but when faced with his first balance sheet, felt like he was seeing double! We had no idea what it took to do business anywhere, and here we were with a promise from God that we would be supporting ministers all over the world.

Yeah right... a tradesman and me, with a high school certificate. Turns out that if you take what you have, God can do the impossible. We should not have been surprised – the Lord took some sand and made man out of it – surely He could take our fire and transform it into something we could use to bless others with!

One step at a time, the Holy Spirit taught and led us. He took us around the loopholes (before we even knew what a loophole was) and in the end established businesses in more than one country, and bank accounts across the world through which to filter finances to those that need it.

If there is a document that needs to be found and signed, you can be sure that the Holy Spirit will lead Craig to find and sign it. If there is a shortcut needed, you can be sure that I will get a dream, stumble onto a webpage, or find a book that gives me the answer I need.

With so many different business institutions and currencies, we have learned the cheapest and easiest ways to move money around. Through great skill and intellect? No! Through great ignorance and tremendous wisdom that comes from God alone.

God is raising up His apostles today in the marketplace and many make the mistake of thinking that they need to know more of the world to become successful. Success tactics are not new in the world or church. So why not do some counter insurgence warfare?

> ### KEY PRINCIPLE
>
> Instead of doing business the "obvious" way – do something new that the devil does not expect. Use wisdom instead of force!

Just like I shared in my illustration at the beginning. The enemy has his battle lines and his bright red coats! Why not be like the Boers and fight this war from behind a rock and along the way?

Do things differently – do them with God's wisdom!

LUCIFER – RELIGIOUS SYSTEMS

> *Isaiah 14:12 How you are fallen from heaven, O Lucifer, son of the morning! How you are cut down to the ground, You who weakened the nations!*
> *13 For you have said in your heart: I will ascend into heaven, I will exalt my throne above the stars of God; I will also sit on the mount of the congregation on the farthest sides of the north:*

At the core of every attack, stands Lucifer's core desire.

> *Luke 4:6 And the devil said to Him, All this authority I will give You, and their glory; for this has been delivered to me, and I give it to whomever I wish.*
> *7 Therefore, if You will worship before me, all will be Yours.*

It was for this reason that he rebelled against God and it is for this reason that he rules all the religious systems of the world.

He is the kingpin of all the religions of the world. You can see his work when the world is tolerant to every religion except that of Christianity. Nothing fishy about that at all (Yeah right!)

In an age of "tolerance" satan is puffed up and worshipped in the form of Buddha, Muhammad, and various other deities. It's a sad state though, when he has to keep coming up with new religions to get man to worship him, when Jesus just needs Christianity to win the race every time! It must drive satan nuts that we adore our Savior with all our heart and mind out of our free will, while his subjects bow in fear and obligation.

So, he is the one who attacks you through the church. He was driven by jealousy thousands of years ago, and thrown down from heaven. That jealousy is still rife, and if he cannot destroy the Church, you can be sure he will try to divide it.

He incites those that are probably the closest to you: other believers, and the church. You rose up and you were much like David in the courts of Saul. You found a place to belong and you thought, "This is it. I can be used of God. I can pour out."

Then, out of nowhere, a javelin barely misses your head before impaling itself in the wall behind you. You think, "What did I do? I was just doing the work of God. I am strumming on my harp and having a good time, and now Saul is trying to kill me. What is up with that?"

That is called an attack from Lucifer. He will use the religious systems to attack you. What has always opposed the moves of God the most? The world? No, the attacks always came from the religious system.

Jesus was opposed by the Pharisees. It was the same religious system that beheaded Paul and crucified Peter upside down. It was not the Gentiles that condemned Jesus – it was His own. There is no greater pain than that. There is no greater reason to walk away from the call or to give satan what he wants.

He craves the worship that the Father gets. He delights in seeing the work of God fighting amongst itself.

You will be going along and the Lord will start bringing you people and then the enemy will send someone to ask you, "Who is your covering? Who are you answerable to? Why should these people come to you?"

You may have people coming to you for ministry, and then the status quo will speak into their ears saying, "You should not trust that guy. He is not under a proper covering."

You get attacks from people that should be standing with you.

We see it through the entire history of the church. Whether you were Pentecostal or Baptist, each of them was persecuted by the next big move. The Catholics killed the reformers. The reformers drowned the Baptists. Look again - that persecution was led by Lucifer himself.

ATTACK FROM PHARISEES

The first attack that Lucifer will levy at you will be through the Pharisees. Good old Saul of Tarsus, who thought he was doing the work of God by persecuting the church, but actually he was satan's advocate. He was doing the work of the enemy, but in his heart, he thought that he was doing God's work.

However, what happened? The church began to pray for him and when they prayed, he turned around and was used of the Lord. That is what you need to realize. In the heart of God's people, they do not think that they are doing the wrong thing.

> ### KEY PRINCIPLE
>
> They do not think that they are tearing you down. They really feel that their zeal is of the Lord. Perhaps, some of their zeal is of the Lord, but satan has pushed them beyond what God intended for them.

You need to stop and pray because these are not unbelievers coming against you. You can say, "Lord, I commit this whole thing to you. Satan, you let God's people go."

Yes, there are times when you are going to have to stand against negative words and judgments that have been spoken over you. It can get really ugly. Warfare is not pretty because satan has licensed people against you and it is bringing persecution.

He twists the Word and they are so bound in their religious thinking that they cannot think any other way. You cannot change every Pharisee in a day. It is going to take time to change their minds.

When these attacks come, you do not sit and have a pity party. When you are in the middle of warfare, you do not go sit in the middle of the battlefield, cross your legs, pout, and say, "It's not fair. The enemy is attacking. What am I going to do?"

You are going to get yourself killed that way! When you see the warfare coming, it is time to pick up your sword and stand against it.

It is for you to see that this attack is coming from a higher level than a few misinformed individuals. This is satan trying to discourage you from the direction that God has given you.

So what is the solution here?

> *Proverbs 25:21 If your enemy is hungry, give him bread to eat; and if he is thirsty, give him water to drink;*
> *22 For so you will heap coals of fire on his head, and the Lord will reward you.*

KEY PRINCIPLE

The ultimate COIN warfare against religious attacks? Love!

I love this passage in Proverbs, because the last thing you want to do with a hungry enemy is feed him! When someone has been standing against you and talking behind your back, you do not want to give them water!

The same person who said such nasty things about you to others is the same that will come to you needing a favor or wanting something from you. Here is a perfect opportunity for you to rub salt in the wound and to make them pay the price.

Yes... you could do that. Or... you could heap coals of fire on their head. You could pick up the weapons that Lucifer uses to destroy and cast down, or you could level this playing field.

Lucifer has been using people and circumstances to shake you. Now it is your turn to strike back. How will you do it? Will you slay the enemy until he lies dead at your feet? If you want true victory, now is the time to feed him.

If he slapped you, you turn the other cheek. Did he steal your coat? Give him your shirt also. Did he trick you into walking a mile? Then walk two. Satan has no comeback for this kind of warfare.

Dare to engage in a strategy of war unknown to satan? Walk in love – gets him every time!

A LITTLE BIT OF SAND...

When Lucifer moves, he does so as an angel of light. His presence in the Church is like a teaspoon of sand in a cake batter. Looking at the cake, it will have every appearance of a tasty treat. Take a bite and it will turn your teeth on edge.

Why destroy the Church when he can just corrupt it? You see, satan tried just wiping the Church out at the beginning. He took away their houses and threw them to the lions. Making martyrs of them only made us stronger. So there is another way.

INFILTRATION OF THE WORLD

Instead of restricting them, he could give them the appearance of prosperity. He could give each man the recognition he craved. Instead of taking away money, he could give the man, with the love of money, a golden calf to bow down to.

There is only one evil greater than poverty in the church and that is prosperity in the Church. We speak so often of our inheritance and I pray that God sets His people free financially. However, I also wonder if the love of money continues to run rampant if this blessing would cause us to be a city on a hill, or an alleyway of vanity and greed?

I have watched first hand what it looks like when finances begin pouring into a ministry. Essentials are no longer to feed the poor or to support the work of God. It is rather for the latest lighting and carpeting to compete with the Church next door.

I wonder how Paul would feel walking into many of our churches today fresh from one of his beatings. With bruises on his wrists from the iron shackles and his back ripped open from the lashings he received from speaking the word of God – I wonder how he would look on us in our era of prosperity?

The church complains of lack time and again. We struggle against the pressures of the world – but what is our purpose here? Is it truly to do the work of God or to prove to the world that we have "made it?" Would you have what it takes to join Apostles Paul and Peter on a tour of their churches?

Shipwrecked and floating days in the ocean, would you have the grace to shake off a poisonous snake and go on to heal and then evangelize an entire island? Or would you sit in a corner complaining about how cold it is and how "unfair" life is because you have never driven a new car before?

Yes, we have a watered down Gospel that laughs all the way to the bank. And there stands Lucifer as he watches the world contaminate the Church and makes it lukewarm.

VICTORY OVER LUCIFER

There is only one way to beat the world in the Church.

> *Romans 12:1 I beseech you therefore, brethren, by the mercies of God, that you present your bodies a living sacrifice, holy, acceptable to God, which is your reasonable service.*
> *2 And do not be conformed to this world, but be transformed by the renewing of your mind, that*

*you may prove what is that good and acceptable
and perfect will of God.*

Ah yes... you know where I am going with this. You are
a prophet after all, where else did you think you would
find your victory? Did you think that by entertaining
the world you could beat it? No prophet of God, it is
when we yield ourselves up as a living sacrifice that we
crucify the flesh and allow the Word of God to ring
through.

KEY PRINCIPLE

> Once your passions are turned
> towards the things of the Lord
> instead of the things of this world,
> you will begin to gain momentum.

Why is it that the Lord could bless Solomon so much? It
was because wealth was the last thing from his mind
when he prayed.

He prayed for wisdom and God entrusted him with
wealth. In the end, it was not wealth that turned
Solomon from God – it was his love of many women. It
was the fact that he opened his heart to Gentile
women and disobeyed the Lord by worshipping other
gods.

Do you understand now why the Lord has challenged
you regarding your finances during your prophetic

training? He has been putting all your flesh and love of money on the cross. When your cravings turn to the latest desire of the flesh, you can be sure that the anointing will begin to wane in your life.

Does the Lord desire to bless you? Of course He does! He just wants to do it His way. He wants to grant you the desires of your heart because He loves you – not because you demand it. I will leave you with one last passage that will give you focus regarding finances. It holds the secret to walking in prosperity... God's way!

> *Luke 12:30 For all these things the nations of the world seek after, and your Father knows that you need these things.*
> *31 But seek the kingdom of God, and all these things shall be added to you.*

THE PROPHETIC SUPER SPY

CHAPTER 02– THE PROPHETIC SUPER SPY

There is no greater COIN warfare than sneaking behind enemy lines and setting the captives free. As a prophet, you are God's "secret spy" finding the cracks in satan's walls and finding a way to reach those he has bound.

As you rise up in your prophetic authority, you will find yourself surrounded by so many who have been bound their entire lives by the work of the enemy. You will see believers crippled by spirits of infirmity.

You will look over a wasteland that once shone as a solid marriage – now lying crumbled in ruins through an attack of strife and vainglory. You will wander into the darkest places and find King's kids feeding on the slime of lust and love of money.

Contaminated with bitterness and bound by power demons, you will be led to believers who have offered up their walk of salvation to eat with pigs. Prophet of God, you are beginning to see your calling take place in front of your eyes.

I have taught you to flow in the gifts of the Spirit. You have learned how to hear God in many ways. You have been armed to do spiritual warfare of every level. You are trained, clothed in armor and your heart has been tried in the fire.

You are ready. Soon you will learn what it means to carry the Prophetic Key of authority and unlock doors on behalf of the Church. For now, though, I want to lead you by the hand through an essential function of the prophet.

What is the purpose of all this anointing and authority if you do not use it for others? So you have proved that God speaks to you. So what? So you have overcome the flesh. So what?

What about the sick, broken and bruised half dying all around you? You have engaged in spiritual warfare on the battlefield. Now, let me show you what it means to truly engage in COIN warfare.

It's time to get to the nitty-gritty and get into people's lives. You will find them in satan's dungeons chained to prison walls, guarded by ruler demons. Men and women of God demonized and without hope of the future.

Remember what I shared regarding Lucifer's desire to split the Church? Using the systems of the world is just one of his tactics. The other is to get believers to invite him. You will not believe how many believers are demonized in the Church today.

Perhaps I was naïve – but I did not expect demon manifestations from those I was training. Well that naiveté sure left quickly when I experienced one manifestation after another as God moved in our meetings.

DEMONIC BONDAGE

In ministry, you are going to find so many of God's people bound by the enemy. Some will be bound in cycles of sin, or fear, that cripples them. Others will be in an even worse state and will be bound by possessing demons. In the chapters that follow I am going to teach you how to handle both kinds of oppression.

DEMONIC OPPRESSION VS. DEMONIC POSSESSION

Doing warfare in the heavenly realm opens doors in the natural realm. It will prepare the hearts of God's people and arrange circumstances for the Kingdom spies to make their way into the enemy's camp.

Often, you as the prophet, will be one of those spies. You will be the one sneaking in and removing satan's bondage from the elect. Now even in the world, when a force goes in to rescue a prisoner of war, they have to be prepared for anything.

It is not uncommon that if someone that has been in bondage for a long time, they are so used to being turned towards the cause of the enemy, that instead of being happy at being set free, they will turn on their own.

In the same way, it is essential that you understand the difference between demonic oppression and possession, because you will need to treat each one differently. Some rules remain the same for both though.

In both cases, the blood of Jesus is the solution. In both cases, repentance removes the license that satan has been given in their lives.

However, things differ greatly when it comes to the manifestation of that oppression. The difference also lies on how the person came under that bondage in the first place. Once you understand the difference, you will also know where to begin in helping to smash the chains that have them bound.

DEMONIC OPPRESSION

> *Acts 10:38 How God anointed Jesus of Nazareth with the Holy Spirit and with power, who went about doing good and healing all who were oppressed by the devil, for God was with Him.*

Strong's Concordance for the Word Oppressed:

2616 - katadunasteuo {kat-ad-oo-nas-tyoo'-o}

AV - oppress 2; 2

1) to exercise harsh control over one, to use one's power against one
2) to oppress one

Simply put, demonic oppression is the result of the enemy being the bully that he is! Remember how you learned in the *Prophetic Warrior* that the enemy has 3 battlefields?

He attacks in the battlefield of the soul, the circumstances and the systems of this world. A soldier can only fight the good fight for so long, before their knees get weak. Even Samson, after killing all the Philistines with the jawbone of a donkey, was terribly weak after the event.

When you have been facing one attack after the other from the enemy, your arm gets weak. If you do not have a team, or others to help pick you up, you will find yourself faltering. Sooner or later you will become discouraged.

You will begin to believe the stones of accusation being thrown at your window. Eventually, one of those stones will break through. The continual attack on your circumstances will start to erode your faith and hope.

Before you know it, you have allowed satan license and have given into his attacks. You have allowed fear to grip you. You entertain the voices of accusation. You steal a moment to taste the gall of bitterness. You, child of God, are now in the throes of oppression.

> **KEY PRINCIPLE**
>
> Simply put – demonic oppression is the continual attack of the enemy that you eventually submit to.

That is what Acts 10:38 is talking about. In the Strong's Concordance, the word "oppression" means to exercise harsh control over. The enemy will keep attacking you until he has gained the upper hand. A wrestling match, where he eventually overcomes you.

From there, your mind is all over the place and you find it hard to take God at His Word.

> *Luke 11:34 The lamp of the body is the eye. Therefore, when your eye is good, your whole body also is full of light. But when your eye is bad, your body also is full of darkness.*
> *35 Therefore take heed that the light which is in you is not darkness.*

What was light is, now darkness. Your eye no longer sees the truth. Fear has eaten up your faith, bitterness, your love, and self-pity has consumed your hope. The light is snuffed out and it feels that the only light you have left, is darkness.

This is what oppression looks like and it is the easiest to help someone overcome.

SINS OF THE HEART

Sins of the heart are what allows satan this kind of control in our lives. The kind of control that manipulates your mind, emotions, and will. This kind of oppression confuses the mind, spikes wrong emotions, and leads to sinful and willful actions.

Someone under demonic oppression will not manifest in the same way as someone that is possessed. Instead their minds will be bound. They will struggle with things like a spirit of anger, and continual fear.

Power demons arrayed against them on every side, making so much noise that they cannot hear the Lord. In this moment, they will allow their flesh to dominate their decisions instead of their spirit.

The *Prophetic Warrior* book is all about demonic oppression and how you encounter it as a prophet. So I am not going to labor it here.

The point is, once you understand this difference, you will be ready for the next chapter, where I will teach you how to help someone in this spiritual condition.

DEMONIC POSSESSION

> *Acts 16:16 Now it happened, as we went to prayer, that a certain slave girl possessed with a spirit of divination met us, who brought her masters much profit by fortune.*

Strong's Concordance for the Word Possessed:

2192 - echo {ekh'-o}

> AV - have 613, be 22, need + 5532 12, misc 63, vr have 2; 712

> 1a) to have (hold) in the hand, in the sense of wearing, to have (hold) possession of the mind

(refers to alarm, agitating emotions, etc.), to hold fast keep, to have or comprise or involve, to regard or consider or hold as

2) to have i.e. own, possess

2b) used of those joined to any one by the bonds of natural blood or marriage or friendship or duty or law etc., of attendance or companionship

4) to hold one's self to a thing, to lay hold of a thing, to adhere or cling to

4a) to be closely joined to a person or a thing

There is a word that keeps cropping up when you look at the Strong's Concordance translation of the word "possession," can you spot it?

You will see that in more than one place, possession is referred to as ownership. There is a drastic difference between being oppressed by the devil, and being possessed by the devil. Unfortunately, it is all lumped together and then you wonder why people do not break free!

> ### KEY PRINCIPLE
>
> The most outstanding difference between oppression and possession is that oppression comes from submitting to the continual attack of the enemy. Possession results from giving satan ownership of your body.

How do you give satan ownership? I knew you were going to ask that. It is a lot simpler than you might imagine, and when you see it for yourself, many things are going to fall into place. The secret lies in this passage,

> *1 Corinthians 6:16 Or do you not know that he who is joined to a harlot is one body with her? For the two, He says, shall become one flesh.*
> *17 But he who is joined to the Lord is one spirit with Him.*
> *18 Flee sexual immorality. Every sin that a man does is outside the body, but he who commits sexual immorality sins against his own body.*

The Word tells us that we are to present our bodies as a living sacrifice to the Lord. When we do this, we give the Holy Spirit license in our lives. In essence... He takes possession of who we are, and we become His temple.

Now, think about this for a moment. What if you yielded your body as a living sacrifice to satan? You can see where I am going with this...

> ### KEY PRINCIPLE
>
> Demonic possession is the result of yielding your body up to the service and worship of satan.

I love what it says in 1 Corinthians 6. When you give your body up to a prostitute, you are making yourself one with her! This is why the Word speaks so much about fleeing prostitution.

It is not just a case of being sinful – but the fact that when you deliberately yield up your body to satan, you give him ownership of it.

Think about it. When you engage in bitterness, you give satan license in your soul. He uses this license to manipulate your thoughts and emotions.

When you give satan license in your body through sins of the flesh, you give him license to possess and manipulate it. So when you are in praise and worship and someone manifests a demon and starts crawling around on the floor as a snake... you are seeing someone who gave license to satan through a sin of the flesh.

If you are praying with someone and they are so bound by fear that they cannot hear the Lord any longer, you are ministering to someone that is oppressed through sins of the heart. As you make this distinction, you just strapped a new sword to your side.

You will come to learn as a prophet that you will not always use the same kind of weapon. Sometimes you will use a sword, and other times, a dagger. Know which weapon to use for what.

So what kind of sins of the flesh are we talking about here? Does this mean that if I swear at my boss behind her back that I am going to wake up tomorrow morning possessed by Lucifer himself?

Relax. It takes a bit more than that! In fact, the Word lays it out so clearly for us and when I point out exactly what sins of the flesh lead to possession, it will become clear.

On a side note, are you already beginning to see why possessing demons can't just jump from one person to another? If you cast a demon out of someone who was just hissing on the floor, that demon cannot just hop, skip and jump to the next passerby and go on his merry way.

No, there are clear rules to follow. The spiritual realm has its own structure and even the enemy cannot just take what has not been given to him. So let's see exactly what gives him ownership and from there... learn how to take it away!

SINS OF THE FLESH

> *Galatians 5:19 Now the works of the flesh are evident, which are: adultery, fornication, uncleanness, lewdness,*
> *20 idolatry, sorcery, hatred, contentions, jealousies, outbursts of wrath, selfish ambitions, dissensions, heresies,*
> *21 envy, murders, drunkenness, revelries, and the like; of which I tell you beforehand, just as I also told you in time past, that those who practice such things will not inherit the kingdom of God.*

I told you the Word makes it clear! Want to see what sins of the flesh lead to possession? Take a look at the works of the flesh and you will begin to see the core of how man gives his body up to satan as a living sacrifice.

You see, that is the point of each of these sins – they are not just incorrect choices. These sins are not just mistakes or misunderstandings. Each of these sins deliberately yields the body into satan's service.

When you got saved, you submitted your spirit, soul, and body to the Lord. You made him your master. Now when man submits his body to satan, he makes satan his master.

Let us not even talk of the confusion a Christian faces when he has not fully taken away the ownership he gave satan!

I have taken the passage above and broken it down into five sins of the flesh that give satan ownership of your body, and so lead to demonic possession. I am taking advantage of the fact that at this stage of your training, you are secure enough in yourself to go through each of these points and to apply the ones to your life that are valid to your situation.

Although I used the personal pronoun "you" throughout the remaining chapter, I am not personally accusing you of sleeping with prostitutes or of beating up your spouse. Seriously... I have had people get mad at me, because they read a book and complained that I accused them of things that did not apply. (Yeah, I also shook my head in disbelief.)

However, on the rare chance that you are a "touchy feely" type and easily offended allow me to provide a disclaimer. I bring up some sensitive subjects below and just because I use the word "you" does not mean it all applies to your life.

Allow the anointing to penetrate your heart. Allow the principles to sink into your spirit. If something I say hits you like a spear in the side and you flinch... well then prophet, I have but one question to ask you, "What on earth are you doing off the cross?!"

IDOLATRY

> *1 Corinthians 10:14 Therefore, my beloved, flee from idolatry.*

> *1 Corinthians 10:20 Rather, that the things which the Gentiles sacrifice they sacrifice to demons and not to God, and I do not want you to have fellowship with demons.*
> *21 You cannot drink the cup of the Lord and the cup of demons; you cannot partake of the Lord's table and of the table of demons.*

This is by far the most common way that someone becomes possessed by a demon. If someone worships satan, he will take ownership. It stands to reason – you signed a contract with him that read, "I give my life over to you."

When you get born again, you give ownership to the Lord, but it is essential in this time to make it clear to satan that you are changing sides! This is what Paul meant when he spoke about having two masters.

You cannot give both God and satan ownership of your body! Sure, when you get born again, you have submitted your spirit to God. Your spirit is recreated in Christ. However, did you also revoke the license you gave to satan, if you ever willingly served him through false religion?

The kind of idolatry I am talking about here is something all of us can agree on. Witchcraft, Mormonism, Jehovah's Witness, Wicca, News Age Cult, palm reading... it's a long list.

How about spiritual impartations you received from someone who was demonized? Crazy as it sounds, I have seen children of God looking up to a leader whose physical manifestation is misunderstood as the work of the Holy Spirit instead of the demon it is!

They crave the same manifestation thinking that it will draw them closer to God. They open themselves up wide to the influence. Asking for it. Praying for it, and so receiving it.

The point is, when you submit yourself to satan and worship him in any way, you give him possession. When someone who has been involved in the occult gets born again, it is essential to have them renounce that old contract!

I have seen this a lot in my lifetime because of the strong ancestral worship that is found in South Africa. Many are brought up worshipping the ancestors and demons. Getting born again is not enough – they have to renounce their old ways. If they do not do this, they will remain possessed and when things get tough, they will go to their witch doctors for cures.

If you grew up in a family that engaged in the occult, dealing with it is so simple. Rip up that old contract. You see, dealing with demons does not have to be all intense and all super duper.

So you gave him license. Well take it back! How hard is that? Never forget, God gave man a free will! What kind of staying power does satan have over someone he possesses?

Jesus died and His blood leaves a stain so strong that no demon in hell can counter it. What does satan have? He has only sin to keep us anchored. He has no blood to keep us. He has no power to sustain us, and the death he uses to bring fear was overthrown by Christ.

So no... satan does not have a permanent hold on any man! While Jesus could boast that no one could snatch us from His hand, satan has to reduce himself to guile and trickery to keep man serving him.

No matter what contract you made with satan, the only thing that keeps him anchored is sin. Well now... we are prophets... we know what to do with sin, don't we?

SEXUAL IMMORALITY

Why sexual immorality? Well just like the Word says, when you have sex with someone, you become one with them. In other words, you enter into a blood covenant with them. You yield your body up to them as a sheep to the slaughter.

We spoke in *Prophetic Warrior* about sexual abuse and sin. Sexual abuse most certainly leads to oppression. The spiritual link with the abuser causes your mind, emotions, and will to come under serious attack.

However, when you wake up one day and decide to engage in sexual debauchery for yourself, is the day that you offer your body to satan for his evil purpose.

The moment you decided to have that homosexual affair, you worshipped satan with your body.

The moment you decided to sleep around, you offered your body up, through a covenant act, to the enemy. You gave him ownership.

Being attacked with thoughts of lust is oppression. Engaging in pornography and joining your body to someone you should not, leads to possession.

From there, it feels as if your body is not your own. You might not slither on the floor like a snake (although some have!) but lust will control you to the point of destroying your marriage.

You will lust after those you should not and struggle with every other work of the flesh. Your sin will feel uncontrollable... and what is the fruit? Satan is glorified in your broken marriage and torn relationships. You made a contract of blood and that possessing demon has ownership of you.

When trying to minister to someone with uncontrollable issues with lust, realize that you are dealing with possession. Deal with the sin. Deal with the demon. Help them gain the victory.

HATRED (ABUSIVE ANGER)

A child grows up seeing his father beat his mother. After years of taking the abuse himself, his mind is warped with a strange sense of how to deal with conflicts. He is oppressed by the enemy.

The day he chooses to raise his hand in hatred or in anger, he offers his body up willingly to what he knows is wrong. Have you ever seen anyone possessed with a demon of anger?

It is not the most pleasant experience - I can tell you! Personally, I do not think that "anger" is a strong enough word. I prefer the word "hate" because that is exactly what it looks like.

The Lord tells us to be angry and not to sin, but hate is something else all together. It is an uncontrollable anger that has been given over to the enemy. When you deliberately decide to use violence to solve your problems, you give your body up as a living sacrifice to the enemy.

You allow the hatred within to drive you, and as you do that, you give satan a place he should never have. Now you are trying to serve the Lord, and you find yourself doing things you should not.

You find yourself raising your hand in anger when you should not. You walk away ashamed, wishing that you had more self-control. Yes, you need self-control, but first you need to deal with that possessing demon!

It is a lot more than just bad judgment calls now. Perhaps it was a poor choice at the beginning. A deliberate sin that you chose to engage in that has now evolved to something else. Anger and bitterness turned to hatred, and you used that force to get your way and beat others down both physically and psychologically.

As you let this principle drive home, you become armed with yet another weapon of warfare.

Knowing the truth sets you free! If you are ministering to someone that is struggling with uncontrollable sin that seems to "take them over," you now know what you are dealing with! You are dealing with a possessing demon and you need to go back to the time that they gave it license.

DRUG USE (DRUNKENNESS)

I have yet to minister to anyone who took drugs and not have had to deal with demons. Taking narcotics or using alcohol to the point of becoming an alcoholic, delivers up their body to the enemy.

Not only do drugs help the user to enter into a spiritual state, but they are experiencing that state without Christ. They go in uncovered, and they go in having given their bodies to the enemy.

If you are ministering to someone who was a drug user, I promise, you have a possessing demon to deal with. Not only did they yield up their bodies, but their spirit as well through the experience.

MANIFESTATION OF OPPRESSION VS. POSSESSION

I am going to list just a few points on how to identify demonic oppression versus possession. It is quite obvious for the most part, but let us summarize what you have learned so far! Note that someone will not necessarily display all of the points at once. However, once you minister to them, it will be quite clear which category they fall into.

Oppression	Possession
• Attacks on the mind • Emotions out of control • Confusing thoughts • Struggle with fear and guilt • Sense of feeling overwhelmed • Nightmares • Inner striving and conflict	• Physical manifestations (demon might speak through person's lips) • Uncontrollable sinful actions • Uncontrollable anger • Uncontrollable lying • Uncontrollable lust

OVERCOMING OPPRESSION

CHAPTER 03 – OVERCOMING OPPRESSION

Imagine that you have broken enemy lines and pulled the prisoners of war out of the enemy's dungeon.

Is it enough to break their chains and then leave them to fend for themselves? No! They need to be fed, clothed, healed and settled back into society. Your job is not done until you have given them something to displace that demon.

Your job is not done until you have ministered healing and taught them how to hear the voice of Jesus for themselves. Now you already know how to minister inner healing – how about I get on with it and teach you how to deal with those demons?

SIN HURTS

Every toddler goes through a phase of curiosity. They discover the world through touch and taste... putting their hands into everything they can. My second daughter Jessica took this phase to a whole new level.

We were at a nice dinner, with candles on the table for atmosphere. Jessica just wanted to touch that candle.

I knew that if she touched the flame, she would get hurt. So, I would say, "Do not touch the flame, my lovey."

You know where this is going. I turned around for just one second and without remorse, she put her hand on that flame and burnt herself. Tears followed and I am not sure who felt worse – Jessica with her burn, or me for not being quick enough.

Regardless of the right or wrong of the situation, there was no doubt that in that moment, when she reached out and touched it, she made a choice.

She did not do that again. In fact, she steered clear of candles for some time after that because she knew that when she touched them, they bit back!

That is how it is when it comes to demonic oppression. Each of us have a choice to make. Nobody walks along the road innocently, when out of nowhere, a candle jumps on them, leaving a nasty burn. It does not happen that way and neither does it happen that way in the spiritual realm.

NO ONE IS A VICTIM

Sin always opens the door. The problem with thinking that people are victims is that it takes away hope for you and for them.

What are you going to do? Are you going to gang up on the demon and tell it to go? You are going to waste a lot of time doing that.

Have you never seen this before? You pray with someone and bind the work of the enemy and then in a month, week, or a little bit down the line, you are back to square one, dealing with the same problem again.

You are going to deal with the same demon again and again. Why? It is because that person has a free choice and they have made the wrong choice. Until they come to a point where they are ready to make the right choice, there is nothing that you can do about it.

KEY PRINCIPLE

> Sin always opens the door. The problem with thinking that people are victims is that it takes away hope for you and for them.

The encouraging thing about knowing this is that it brings hope. It means that there is a solution. How can you give someone hope by saying, "Shame, you are a poor victim. You cannot help it that you are oppressed"?

They will never get set free that way. It is not nice to hear the truth, which is that you are responsible for what is going on in your life. If there is one message that I have to bring to everyone that I work with, it is that they are responsible.

They are not a victim of their circumstance. They are not a victim of their demon. There came a time, just like when my daughter looked at that flame and said, "Should I listen to mommy or should I do it anyway?"

THE CONSEQUENCES OF SIN

She reached out her hand and grabbed that flame and she paid the price for her sin. I could be there to help her to fix it, but the point is that I could not undo what she had done.

She burned herself and I could not take that away from her. I could only try to make it better afterwards.

It is the same when you disobey the Word of God. It is like making a deliberate choice to put your hand in the fire. You know the Word. You know what is wrong or right. Yet, you do what is wrong anyway. You are going to get burnt.

They were not just walking along and some demon jumped on them and took hold of them. They might be caught up in consequences that satan is using to the utmost, but they are the one that allowed curiosity to lead them into satan's grounds.

If you try to help someone with that kind of thinking, you are going to get a backlash and you are not going to sleep that night. You are going to come under a heavy attack.

Below I am going to give you some very easy steps and two main rules that you need to remember. I have dealt a lot with how to help people overcome, so I will be brief.

I am only going to give you the basic rules and steps because I want you to keep the facts in your mind. There are two main rules. Underline or write them down so that you can remember them.

Also keep in mind that I am talking specifically about oppression right now. I will walk you through dealing with possession in the next chapter. So if you are itching to get into casting out demons, then you will just need to be patient and follow me through these steps first. (Prophets always like to jump ahead to the fun and dramatic stuff!)

RULE #1 – THEY MUST ASK FOR HELP

Whether someone is battling with a spirit of lust, bitterness, or whatever the bondage is, no matter how clear and obvious it is to you, until they ask for help, do not help. Do not impose your ministry. You are going to end up in trouble.

You would think that anyone under the load of oppression would want help! Well Moses thought he would try to help those two Israelites after killing the Egyptian and he got a backlash. It took those people 40 years before they started asking for help.

The best thing to do in such a situation is to go find a burning bush and to take care of the goats you already have! Leave that person in God's hand.

Now what if the person under that oppression is a spouse or someone you are discipling? Well then you start off by giving it to the Lord! If they are open, you can offer your help – but be a bit savvy with this one. Learn to identify if they are just "going along with it" or if they really want some help.

If the person that is under oppression is someone under your leadership and their sin is effecting others, then you have every right to address that sin. You do not have a right to minister to them though! That is really up to them.

Now I know how you feel. You see them going for that wall and you want to help so badly! I understand! It is the heart that God has given you for His people. The thing is, you will damage them and take on some hurt yourself if you do not wait until they are ready.

Keep praying. Keep watching their back and wait until they really want your help!

RULE #2 – THEY MUST MEAN BUSINESS

This is tricky. It does not mean that just because they ask for help that they mean business. A lot of people say, "I cannot believe that I got burnt."

However, if you give them another chance, they will have their hand in the fire quick as a flash again. They need a conviction and be willing to deal with sin in their life.

You are not going to get a breakthrough with someone that always has an excuse for their sin. I cannot tell you how exhausting it is to try and minister to someone that responds to every glaring sin with,

"My mother did it."

"My father did it."

"It was because of how my parents treated my sister that I am so bitter."

"My first girlfriend cheated on me. That is why I struggle with lust."

"I was abused, that is why I sleep around now."

If they ask for help and their idea of help is getting to spew all their bitterness and frustration over you - they do not mean business.

"I had an affair and now I am in a bad situation. My marriage is in a lot of trouble. Can you please pray for me so that the problem will go away?"

There is no doubt in my mind that they want help, but they do not mean business. They want you to pray the consequences of their sin away.

They are not prepared to face the consequences of their sin or prepared to face their sin at all.

Be very conscious of that. Just because someone says, "Please help me," does not mean that they really want help. They have to mean business.

You are not the genie from the lamp from the children's story "Aladdin," who grants three wishes to wipe their problems away. If this is the kind of mentality that they have, then I'm afraid that they are taking their doctrine from the wrong book.

I could help my daughter when she burnt her hand, but I could not take the blister away. It took time to heal. It is the same with God's people. God wants to heal them, but for goodness sake, please be prepared to stop putting your hand in the fire and adding scar to scar!

How to Deal With Sin

It is a happy day when someone comes to you for ministry, wanting help, and ready to do whatever God wants them to do. Deliverance will be easy and healing will follow on naturally. I made a point on the first two rules, because once you have determined that they are ready, you will flow in revelation.

The Lord will only give you revelation according to the person's faith. Now if they do not really want help or mean business, they will not have faith. This means you will not get revelation.

This is so discouraging for any minister. It means you have to go on your knowledge of principles and the

Word alone. You can do little else but speak blessing and give a few words of counsel.

It is much more rewarding to minister to someone who is ready and to receive revelation and minister under the anointing. That is what we are called to do! So take the lead here and follow the steps listed below.

STEP 1 – TAKE AWAY THE LICENSE

It is for this reason that they must mean business. It is because they have to look at themselves and say, "I am responsible."

Submit, confess, resist. The three steps in action once again! Although the enemy came against them like a flood, before you can push it back, you need to seal up the cracks in their castle walls.

Once they can see where they submitted, and allowed the plan of the enemy to overwhelm them, you give them the upper edge.

Identifying the open door is usually quite simple. Ask the person questions such as,

"What was going on in your life when you started feeling this way?"

"Can you identify a moment when these thoughts or nightmares happened?"

Once you can zero in on a time frame for the oppression, where the door was opened is usually quite obvious to the person asking for ministry. Do not forget though... you are a prophet!

Now is the time to ask the Holy Spirit for revelation and to show you were the opening was. You might see a person or sense an emotion that the person has.

Once they identify where they gave in to the enemy, get them to repent and seal up that crack!

STEP 2 – TELL THE ENEMY TO LEAVE

Now we are ready to get this party started!

> Ready to rumble? Check!

> Sin under the blood? Check!

> Ready for some payback? Double check!

It is important that whoever you are ministering to knows the power of repentance and how simple it is. This is not a time to feel condemned, but an opportunity to get the upper hand!

Now that their cracks are sealed, it is time for the devil to get his running shoes on. Do you see what you are doing here? You are doing a lot more than just helping someone break free of oppression... you are equipping them to do good works of every kind!

By taking them through this process correctly, you arm them to handle the same situation anywhere, anytime. Now it is time to resist the devil.

Do not pray for the person, but teach them to take authority over the enemy for themselves. Encourage them by saying that they have the authority in Jesus name. They just put their sin under the blood... satan has no hold on them right now.

It is time to take their ground back! It is important that they address the enemy directly. Do not allow them to get away with, "Lord Jesus please take this away from me..."

When Jesus took authority over demons, He did not say, "Father please cast this demon out..." Instead He said, "Demon! Come out of him!"

Wipe away the fear of the devil. Put the sword back in the hand of that believer.

You might need to help out by showing them how to pray until they get the hang of it.

> "I bind that spirit of fear in Jesus name!"

> "Satan, I take authority over you! You no longer have license through my sin. Now loose your hold on me."

> "I take authority over these thoughts in my mind..."

> "I bind this spirit of lust..."

All in a day's work, prophet. Job well done! You are almost ready to wrap this up and move on to the next soldier of Christ that needs your help.

STEP 3 – FOLLOW UP WITH COUNSEL

Once you have dealt with the spiritual side, you then need to deal with the habits and the circumstance that they are in. They are going to need help. It is one thing to deal with the demon and another thing to heal the blister that has been caused because of the situation.

In the case of a marriage, you are going to need marital counsel. If a husband has a spirit of lust, and he has gone and had an affair, it is great that he prays, confesses his sin, and deals with the demon.

However, there is a lot more going on than just a spirit of lust. They need marital counsel. They obviously have problems.

In times like this, I encourage prophets to work with a pastor or teacher to balance them. While you might get to the root of the problem by the Spirit, learning to apply the Word to the problem correctly requires a different anointing.

In a perfect world, a prophet should be working side by side with a teacher so that they can fill every need. You have dusted this child of God off and dressed them in armor. However, it is going to take a teacher to show them how to use that sword effectively.

If you do not have a teacher or pastor to work with… well then your training is not over yet, is it? Did you think that you could just remain at the same level forever? You will soon come to learn that God will challenge you as you reach prophetic office.

I am already gearing you for the conclusion of this series which will end on the high note of the Prophetic Key. Yes, when you stand in the fullness of office, you will learn how essential it is to understand some doctrine and counseling principles!

For now, though, lead them out of the dungeons of darkness and into the light of Christ. When all is said and done, you might not have done everything perfectly.

That is alright – you can fail on every single point except this one:

Once you are done, make sure that you leave that person in the arms of Jesus. There is just one purpose for breaking this believer out of the kingdom of darkness, and that is to help them realize their place in the Kingdom of God!

> *2 Timothy 3:17 That the man of God may be complete, thoroughly equipped for every good work.*

DEALING WITH POSSESSION

CHAPTER 04 – DEALING WITH POSSESSION

Congratulations! You just learned to set the captives free. Look at you! What do you know? I am starting to see quite the mature prophet standing in front of me.

It is in that moment of, "I think I can do this…" that something crazy usually happens. Something like a dramatic demon manifestation.

Just when you think you have all the principles "down," something will happen to remind you that yes… you are a prophet and yes… this means you live on the cross.

That is what happened to me more than a few times! Going all "prophet" in praise and worship, I am so busy having the time of my life that I often forget that Jesus might love my melody, but that it does tend to send satan through the roof.

There have been times when I picked up my guitar and the anointing just fell! "Glory Hallelujah! More Lord! I praise you Je… what on earth is that yelling all about…?"

"Are you kidding me? Is that a demon manifesting all over my meeting?"

It is difficult, in that moment to say, "Kindly confess your sin so that we can get back to the good stuff."

Doesn't work. The demon will just start yelling at you. There is going to be a whole lot of spitting going on, some yelling, and a couple of other undignified bodily movements. No amount of trying to "make them understand" will stop them from growling and hollering.

So, you need to get this person to calm down. To help you out, I have another three rules to write in your little black book (You keeping track here prophet?).

GET YOUR "PROPHETIC WARRIOR" ON!

When it comes to demons and spiritual warfare, there are so many strange teachings out there.

"This is a super spiritual thing that you have to study for years for."

"You really need to be anointed specifically for this."

"You stay away from it, if you can. If anything happens, you leave it to the professionals."

> *KEY PRINCIPLE*
>
> When we look at how Jesus walked the earth, we begin to see that dealing with demons and spiritual warfare is a part of everyday life as a believer.

> *Mark 16:17 And these signs will follow those*
> *who believe: In My name they will cast out*
> *demons; they will speak with new tongues;*

Is the gift of tongues only for "gifted" believers? No it is for every believer! Can you speak in tongues? Awesome! You can also cast out demons.

We have an enemy that would love to take us out. I think that the greatest lie that satan has brought into the church is that this is something that you cannot tackle yourself. You have to wait for someone else to fight on your behalf.

PUT YOUR FEAR INTO PERSPECTIVE

Why is it that when it comes to God people can treat the Lord like they want and serve Him when they want, but when it comes to the enemy, they are shaking in their boots?

It is as if he is so big and strong that they are too afraid to tackle him, but the Lord Jesus is a lamb that can be kicked around.

We have the picture back to front. The King of kings is the one who is awe inspiring and powerful. It is He that we should fear. The enemy is a dog that yaps at our heels and is easy to crush.

So I want to challenge you to change this mindset in the body of Christ... starting with you! What you will learn here is not just for your benefit. You are learning it so that you can pass this on to the body of Christ.

The Church needs to learn how to engage in spiritual warfare effectively. You have two camps. You have one camp that does not want to touch it because they are too afraid, and you have another camp that just walks around casting demons out of everyone, and see demons in absolutely everything.

They overemphasize demons so much that they forget that Jesus won the battle two thousand years ago. We need to bring balance to the body of Christ and that balance, Mr. Prophetic Spy, starts with you.

RULE #1 – DO NOT PERMIT MANIFESTATIONS

> *Luke 4:41 And demons also came out of many, crying out and saying, You are the Christ, the Son of God! And He, rebuking them, did not allow them to speak, for they knew that He was the Christ.*

I know that some of these deliverance preachers like to make someone who is possessed squirm, vomit, scream, and talk through the person's mouth. It might provide material for a viral YouTube video, but does not exactly help the person whooping like a monkey.

Craig and I were at someone's home, and praise and worship did it again... someone in the meeting started to manifest. We made all the mistakes. Talked to the demon. Struggled and fussed. Eventually the penny dropped, I looked her in the eye and called her by name.

In that moment I felt such a deep peace and love overwhelm me. I felt Jesus' heart for her. I spoke tenderly and saw the look of confusion on that demon's face. The woman came to her senses and we could begin helping her get victory.

Then suddenly behind me (you are not going to believe this) the daughter started shrieking in a high pitch. I was tired. That was quite enough excitement for me for a day.

I just looked at that demon in the face and said matter-of-factly, "No. You can just stop that right now."

The demon just stopped and the lady passed out. Then, she got up and everything was fine. Well "fine" for someone who needed to start dealing with that bondage.

I do not permit manifestations because until you can speak to the person, you are not making any progress. That is the most important thing. You need to speak to the person, not the demon. Jesus always told the demons to keep quite and then promptly sent them packing. Good model for us to follow, I think.

RULE #2 – DO NOT ARGUE WITH DEMONS

I do not like demons and I do not like the devil. I am not called as a believer, as a prophet, or as an apostle, to talk to the devil. I have better things to do with my time.

You can talk to the devil all you like, but it is not going to change the person because they are the key. You do not cast demons out of believers. You cast demons out of unbelievers.

> "Demon, come out."

> "I won't. She is mine."

> "Demon, come out."

> "I won't. She is mine."

Stop arguing. In fact, do not talk to the demon at all. Talk to the person. Cut right pass the demon and talk to the believer. Call them by name.

This might be a bit difficult when they are manifesting and hysterical, but if you speak in love and cut through the manifestation to reach the person, you have reached the key.

As a believer, they have the key to stop it. They have the authority to tell satan to get lost.

So, do not permit the manifestations. Do not allow them to even get started, if you can help it. However, if they do manifest, do not argue.

First, you tell the demon to be quiet.

> "Be silent."

Then, you speak to the person.

> "James, I am talking to you."

The demon keeps on shouting...

> "James, let's sit down and talk about this.
> James, you do not have to accept this."

The demon can carry on and scream, but you be persistent and talk to the person. Do not talk to the demon and do not argue.

If the person is born again, then they are aware of what is going on. If you can do that, you can do it in rest.

If you start arguing with the demon, you are in a fight that you cannot win. Either you cast it out or you get the person to tell it to leave. I lean more towards COIN warfare.

There are many that go around casting demons from believers. I say, engage in COIN warfare – be the prophetic super spy! Teach them how to deal with the devil. That way, they can continue to have the victory long after you have gone home, had a coffee and told your family what a crazy night you just had.

RULE #3 – ON TO VICTORY

Then finally, lead them to victory using confession of sin, and telling the enemy to leave. In other words, you take them through the three steps listed in the previous chapter.

If someone physically manifests a demon, you are not just dealing with a generational curse here. You are looking for a sin of the flesh. A sin where they involved themselves with a sect, false religion, Ouija boards, fortune telling or something like that.

Bring them to a conviction of their sin and then they will tell the enemy to go. Sometimes it can be difficult for them. When helping someone who is possessed, they find it hard to maintain control when they bind the enemy. However, they can do it. They still have the power of will. Stand in agreement with them and back them.

I experienced this exact situation once. Up to the point where she was submitting to the Lord, I felt a strong external oppression.

If you have ever experienced this, you know what I mean. Just before the person manifests, I feel a strong, cold oppression as if the entire air is charged with electricity.

When I felt that oppression I knew what was coming. I thought to myself, "Oh no, I really am not in the mood for demons spitting on me right now."

The lady struggled, but she held on and pushed out the words, "Satan... you... leave."

As she got those words out, I immediately felt the lift in the spirit. She looked up at me and said, "It really is different when you do it right."

She got such a breakthrough. It did not have to come to the point of the demon manifesting.

KEY PRINCIPLE

> Believers hold the key to their own spirit!

Once they have taken away the enemy's license, you can stand in agreement and you will get more revelation about any other open doors in their lives.

You need to follow through with counsel, like I mentioned earlier. In the case of the occult, you need to point them to the Word and help them to realize that that is sin and that they cannot do that.

You need to see if they have things in their home or if they are wearing jewelry that is associated with that stuff. If so, they must get rid of those things. You need to follow it up. It is not good enough just to tell the devil to go.

You must make sure that he is not coming back again because I have found, in cases like this, that the demon hangs around a bit looking for license to get access to them again. So, it is important that they keep strong.

Perhaps, there is a weak point. Maybe there is a certain fear that they have, and every time they give into that fear, they go back into that old thing again. That fear drives them back to taking drugs. The unhealed hurt makes it difficult to not want to get their needs met through the flesh.

It is good that you have dealt with the possessing demon, but now you need to deal with the habit that gave that demon license in the first place.

It is a process. If you are called to be a minister, you are not just blazing in there like a "hotshot" casting out demons. Next week they will just be in bondage again because you did not follow them through.

WHAT IF THEY DO NOT WANT TO BREAK FREE?

Usually, when someone has manifested like that, they are pretty quick to want to deal with their sin and to get a victory because they got the fright of their lives.

However, if they are not willing to look at their sin, you are going to have to break spiritual links with them and pray for conviction. If that person did not repent and tell that devil to leave, your work is not done.

I do not care how many times you told the demon to leave. I do not care how many times you cursed and swore at it.

Until that person has dealt with it, you did not get the victory. I do not even care if it looked like they calmed down. Until they have come to conviction, they did not get the victory.

That is how you deal with someone who is manifesting. It is simple and practical. When you experience it, you are now armed with the knowledge of what to do. That is why you have to learn to put on the whole armor of God.

You have to know that Jesus won this battle two thousand years ago. You have to stand in faith and know the Word. When you speak, you should expect that demon to shut up. When you speak, you should expect that person to respond.

When you say, "Satan, you loose your hold," he should let go.

You need to have the conviction that he will loose his hold. That kind of conviction only comes through the Word. So, do not skip any of the steps and think that you can jump ahead.

You are going to regret it when you come to a situation like this. You will hit the wall and then pull out this book again saying, "What did that crazy woman say again...?"

Well I am not done with you yet. You are a warrior remember? That means when everyone else does 10 push-ups, you do 100! So if you have any aching muscles, walk it off and dive into the next chapter, because there I am going to buff up that spirit of yours with some stealth training.

STEALTH TRAINING – READY TO EXTRACT

CHAPTER 05 – STEALTH TRAINING – READY TO EXTRACT

Do you know those checklists that say, "Check off the ones that apply to you?" I love those. They make things so simple. I guess I could have slapped in a crossword puzzle or two, but that might be taking it a bit too far.

So instead I am going to give you a list of the Do's and Don'ts when it comes to dealing with demonic possession.

If you keep your mind on these, spiritual warfare and dealing with demons, especially in manifestations in others, will be very easy.

DO'S AND DON'TS FOR THE PROPHETIC SPY!

Coupled with these principles and your authority in Christ, you will be a master spy, ready to extract any believer that satan has taken hostage. Get your battle plan drawn up and let's prepare you for what lies ahead.

#1 – DON'T GO AROUND CASTING OUT DEMONS

Don't go casting demons out of everybody, especially when it comes to believers. Jesus did not cast demons out of everyone, just those that manifested and came to Him asking for help.

When the father came to Him and said, "My son has a demon and it throws him into the fire." Jesus went and cast that demon out. However, He did not go casting demons out of everyone that He met.

He did not see demons everywhere He looked. He was always moved with love and compassion. He was always mindful of the person, and not of the demon all the time. I often get the impression that Jesus dealt with the demon quickly so that He could do the real work.

Once He dealt with the demon, He usually followed it up with, "Go and sin no more."

"Take up your bed and walk."

"Your sins have been forgiven."

If you are too demon conscious and walk around casting demons out of people, then you are going to experience some serious backlashes. This is a serious flaw in the mainline deliverance ministries.

They just want to go around casting out demons. Yet, how do you know that that demon was not given license? How do you know that that person does not love that demon?

To Love a Demon

Do you think that just because it is a demon that they do not love it? That demon gives them something. You are foolish. You and I think, "Who would want a demon?" However, that demon gives them something, a strength that they would not ordinarily have.

> ***KEY PRINCIPLE***
>
> Just because a person is aware that they have a demon, doesn't mean that they want to get rid of it.

When I have dealt with people, in regards to deliverance, I have found that until they come to conviction and really do not want that thing, they are not going to break free because that demon gives them something.

Unfortunately, it takes a lot more from them than they realize, but it still gives them something in return. In some cases, the spirit of control that takes a hold of someone, gives them the power and ability to push through and handle rejection.

They can close their heart and people can stand against them and they feel nothing. If you take that demon away, they feel vulnerable. So, do not be so keen to just get rid of their demons because they are manifesting.

I have had people manifest demons and they are still not prepared to give it up. Why? It is because that demon gives them a sense of security. It gives them something that makes them feel safe.

DON'T IMPOSE

So don't impose your ministry on anyone. Just because someone has a demon or because someone is having a bad time, it does not mean that they want your ministry.

I cannot figure it out either. You can see that they are going through Hell and that everything is wrong in their life. They are dying, travailing, and all that and you think, "They must really want help. They must want someone to jump in and save them."

No. They are wallowing in self-pity, they think they are a victim, and they are feeling very sorry for themselves.

I remember a story that my father shared with me. When he was a young man, he battled a lot with hypertension. He was called to go to the army and he had an entire collection of pills.

He managed, at that stage, to get a leave of absence because he was not physically fit, so he could get out of it. Then, he said that he was at an evangelistic meeting and this great evangelist wanted to call him up to the front and pray so that he could be healed.

However, he stood there thinking, "I don't want to be healed. I would rather be sick than to have to go back to the army." I just chuckled when he told me that story.

He used this as an illustration to share with me how this evangelist just thought that he would want to be healed. So, he just dragged him up there to pray for his healing. However, my dad was a young guy that did not want to face the pressures of being in the military and he would rather take his tablets than go back into service.

Sure, since then, he received his breakthrough and the Lord really touched him, but that story really stuck in my mind. I thought, "How many times have we done that to people?"

We assume that they do not want that bondage. We assume that they want to be healed. I remember ministering to a guy that was blind and I thought, "Shame. This must be terrible. He must really want to be healed."

However, when I spoke to him, I said, "You should really believe the Lord for your healing" and he said, "It is ok."

I realized that he did not want to be healed. He like the attention that he got and he liked his little comfort zone. He felt comfortable with who he was. That was crazy. He was blind for goodness sake! Didn't he want to be healed? No, he did not.

I could not fathom it, but it was the reality.

KEY PRINCIPLE

> Do not assume that just because
> someone has a problem that they
> want you to fix it.

Do not impose your ministry on anyone or you are going to get a backlash and horrible surprises.

It sounds crazy, doesn't it? Wake up, because this is the reality. If you go around casting demons out of people, it is going to be like, the sons of Sceva, that tried by saying, "We cast you out in the name of Jesus that Paul preaches about."

The demons said, "We know Jesus and we know Paul, but who are you?" Then those demons attacked them. That is what is going to happen to you, if you go around casting demons out unled.

That person is not ready to let that demon go. So, point number one is to not go around casting out demons. Use a little wisdom.

#2 – DO IDENTIFY THE ENTRANCE POINT

Until you identify how the demon gained access into that person's life, you are getting nowhere fast. It is very easy to see the fruits and the manifestations, but it is not so easy to see the entrance points.

What I am speaking of here relates to believers and not unbelievers. This is a prophetic book, not an evangelistic book (just in case you did not get that).

Evangelists, dealing with unbelievers, have a different rulebook entirely.

An evangelist will tell the demon to come out, especially if it starts manifesting and it is interfering with a meeting.

Consider that psychic woman who kept following Paul around and saying, "These people are coming with a message from the Most High." It said that she followed him around for a few days.

Was Paul nuts? (Clearly the man was a teacher and not a prophet, because every prophetic bone in my body would want to send that demon packing!)

Why didn't Paul turn around and say, "Demon, be gone" on the first day? He thought, "Why bother? It is not my place. She likes her demon and her owners like the demon. It gives them money.

He did not just go around casting out demons. He only did it when it started interfering with the work of God and getting in their way. Then he said, "That's enough. Get lost." Just like that. The demon was out of there.

Keep this point in mind though... he was dealing with an unbeliever. When it comes to dealing with a believer, you see how Simon, the sorcerer, came to

Peter and asked him if he could buy the Holy Spirit with money.

Then, Peter said, "You do not know what spirit you are of." Did he go and cast the demon out of Simon? No. He said, "You better go search your heart and go before the Lord."

Do you see the difference? Peter did not turn around and say, "Come out, demon." That man was clearly possessed because he was a sorcerer before and had not fully broken free. Yet, Peter did not cast the demon out. He told Simon to repent.

That believer needs to repent and deal with that entrance point. I have discussed this with you already.

Find out what the entrance point is. This is where you will have to get revelation.

#3 – DO NOT ASSUME THE ENEMY LEFT

Do not assume that just because they repented, that the enemy left. All you did was close the door. You identified the door and you closed it, but the enemy was running rampant through their house.

They might have prayed, "Father, I sinned. Forgive me." That is good and you have taken away the enemy's license, but you have not told him to leave yet.

Do not assume that just because you repent that the enemy is gone. This is why I shared about the importance of following through.

#4 – DO TELL THE ENEMY TO LEAVE

Do not leave the person at, "I see the entry point right there. I really messed up when I got involved in that group. Lord, forgive me for getting involved in drugs. That was sin. Forgive me for opening the door to the enemy."

Then, you leave and you cannot understand what is wrong and why you are getting a backlash. You did not tell the enemy to leave! You may have closed the door and snatched back the keys, but you did not say, "Be gone, satan."

Jesus was tempted three times. He overcame the enemy and He did not sin, but at the end, He had to say, "Be gone." If Jesus, the Son of God, had to tell satan to "be gone" and He was sinless, do not assume that just because you have repented that the enemy will run away. You have to tell him to get lost.

#5 – DO BREAK SPIRITUAL LINKS

You need to break spiritual links when contamination has come from people. For example, say that a lot of this oppression has come through a generational curse. I have had situations where the parent was involved in Voodoo and they dedicated their child to satan when they were a baby.

They can repent and deal with their own occultist involvement and tell the enemy to go. Afterwards though they need to break spiritual links with their parents. They must break those generational curses. (Please refer to the *Strategies of War* series for more on that)

#6 – DO DEAL WITH IDOLS AND CONTAMINATED OBJECTS

Now we have had people who are a tad extreme with this. I mean us prophets would not get all "black and white" with this. No way we would get extreme... right...?

Needless to say we had a few who said, "We got all of our furniture from our parents, so there are obviously generational curses here." Then, they emptied their entire house of everything and sat and slept on the floor.

That is just a smidge dramatic. We do not have to throw away furniture to get the blessing of the Lord. However, when it comes to objects designed as idols, I suggest getting rid of them.

CRUSH THAT GOLDEN CALF!

Some idols that come to mind are objects such as, crosses, stars of David, Buddha statues, African carvings, pentagram pendants, and so forth.

Certainly if you have something that you receive from your family that has a sentimental value, you can pray over it. You could pray over sentimental items and deal with the contamination, but if it is made as an idol specifically, you need to get rid of it.

It is like the guy that I was speaking to you about that had that jewelry that was made as an idol specifically. His parents blessed it so that it would guard him and watch over him for the rest of his life. The purpose of that jewelry was to be an idol.

When Moses came down and they were worshipping the golden calf, they did not just pray over the golden calf. Moses crushed it and threw it into the river. He got rid of it.

There are times that you can pray over something that is just a normal object, but when something has been used specifically as an idol or if it is an idol in your life, then you need to get rid of it.

I may have received something from someone that is very special to me and every time I wear it or I am near it, I think of them. That is a problem if that person is a negative influence in my life. The object is not necessarily the problem, but my attachment to it is a problem.

It is best to just give these things away. Yet, if it is an actual idol, please do not give this away to someone else and contaminate their life.

TRYING TO REACH GOD THROUGH OBJECTS

Idols like the star of David and especially some cultural Jewish objects tend to be used as idols. As if having them nearby or on you during prayer will draw you closer to the Lord.

We do not need to serve the Lord through prayer shawls and shofars. We serve Jesus and we come to Him in spirit and in truth.

Jesus went to the Samaritan woman at the well and He said to her, "A time is coming when you will not need to go to the temple, the mountain, or anywhere. You will serve the Lord in spirit and in truth."

If that was valid for them, how much more valid is it for us? We do not need to be like Catholics and go through Mary or stand before a cross and try to imagine Jesus hanging there. He is with us all the time.

We do not need objects to reach God. If you are using any of these things, they are idols.

I do not need objects to get into the Lord's presence.

Do you want to get into His presence?

"Welcome, Holy Spirit. Thank you for being here, Jesus."

Yup… there He is.

You do not need an idol to touch God. That is what the Israelites thought when they built the golden calf. That if they could have something to see and touch, that it would draw them to God. Do not make that mistake. If you have any idols in your home, pick them up and get rid of them.

You will be amazed at how much the air lifts and how the curses will stop in your life. I feel the Holy Spirit putting an emphasis on this because the enemy has been subtle and he has brought idols into your life that you do not even realize are there.

No People. I do Not Wear a Crucifix

Watch out especially for religious objects. I do not care if it is the family Bible, the crucifix around your neck, or the cross hanging on the wall. If you think at any time that you need that object to feel closer to the Lord - get rid of it! We serve Jesus who died on the cross. We do not serve the cross.

The cross is an object of pain and humiliation. We do not serve the cross. We serve Jesus. If you need those things to get into His presence, you have a problem in your spiritual life and they are standing as a hindrance.

These things are blocking your spirit and they continually give satan license in your life, which is the scariest part of all. Do you really think that the Israelites were so stupid that they thought they were worshipping a demon when they put up those calves?

They thought that they were worshipping God. Aaron said, "This is Yahweh. This is your God. This is what He looks like."

They really thought they were worshipping God, but they were not. You and I both know what they were worshipping and the same applies to all these religious objects. If there is any house cleaning that I suggest you do, it is to go through your house and get rid of your anointing oils, crucifixes, and things that you think get you closer to God.

These things are a counterfeit from the pit of Hell. They are a deception and they are stealing the real blessing of God from you. You do not need any of those things to get into His presence. You do not need any of these things to be washed by His blood.

You do not need any of these things to walk in His power because we have received that all by His grace. You make the grace of God a joke when you think that you can earn it through things that are made by the hands of man.

That is what the Israelites thought. They thought that they could just obey the law. No. The Word of God says in Hebrews that he that has entered into His rest has ceased from his own works, just as God has from His.

We have ceased from our works because we have received this call, not because we are so righteous and because we do it so well, but because of His grace. I want you to search your heart and I want you to search your home because you are an example to the body of Christ.

If that is what you are following, that is what they are going to follow too. Put it aside and you will sense such liberty and you will come into a real relationship with Jesus. Do you want to touch Jesus? You do not need any object to touch Him. You just need to reach out and you will find Him waiting like an eager Groom waiting to take you into an embrace.

#7 – DO NOT TRY TO TELL THE ENEMY TO LEAVE IN YOUR MIND

Remember that this is the battlefield of the enemy?

"If I think the devil away, he will go away."

No. It does not work like that. If I want my daughters to go and do something, I do not think in my mind, "I want you to go clean your room." I am in for a very disappointing day.

If only hey? Perhaps if I thought hard enough, "I would really love my husband to take me out to dinner tonight so that I do not have to cook." That I will open my eyes to find him standing in front of me with a bunch of roses and a reservation to my favorite restaurant.

Come now prophet, time to get out of the clouds again.

If I need my kids to do something, I have to open my mouth and say, "Get up and clean your room."

My husband would be ever so grateful if I just opened my mouth and said, "Love I am so tired tonight, can we go out for dinner so that I do not need to cook?"

(Some by-the-by marital advice for you ladies out there.)

(Err... gents... don't forget the roses.)

Back to my point – the enemy will not leave if you do not tell him to! You cannot think him away.

"I wish the enemy would go away." Does not make him head for the hills.

We have the authority on our tongue. You need to open your mouth and say, "satan, be gone now."

Since people are so afraid of the whole warfare thing, they are too afraid to open their mouths and say it. When you are ministering to someone, you are going to experience this.

They will be happy to repent to the Lord or to pray anything else, but when it comes to the enemy, they are too afraid. They pray, "Lord, please tell the devil to go away."

Guess what? The Lord was not the one that put him there. Your license through sin did, so why make the Lord do your dirty work for you?

Jesus did not pray on the mount, "Father, please tell the enemy to stop tempting me."

He said, "satan, be gone."

The disciples did the same. They were not afraid to confront satan to his face and tell him, "Get out of here."

You must do the same and when you are ministering to someone else, you must make sure they rebuke the devil out loud and make their stand. Then, they will get the victory.

#8 – Demons Require License Through Sin

I had someone get a hold of me once and say, "I need you to pray with me that circumstances do not get so difficult that I am forced to have to take drugs again."

"Are you serious?"

"Yes, you must pray for me that I do not sin."

They claim to be a victim of circumstance. It is as if they are walking along and suddenly this desire comes upon them and this demon attacks them and they cannot help it, their hands reach out and they take those drugs.

I say, "That is your choice. Isn't it? No demon in Hell can force you to do anything. No one is a victim in this world, certainly not a believer, who knows their authority. That is why teaching the truth is such an important part of deliverance.

They need to know that they are not a victim to sin. Regardless of circumstances, God gave us a free choice. Granted, sometimes those choices are difficult to make, but that is why we need the Holy Spirit!

Be sure to separate sin from circumstance. If someone is demonized, sin gave it license – not circumstance. Circumstances bare pressure on us and make it difficult – but only an open door can give satan license.

Sure, some people do have it harder than others. We should have love and compassion.

KEY PRINCIPLE

> Replace any doctrine that you believe that makes you think that demons just run around jumping into people whenever they want, forcing them to sin against their own will.

If that were true, we would have to throw out most of the New Testament. Peter, Paul and John tell us clearly not to walk in sin. They tell us to put aside the lusts of the flesh and to walk in the light as He is in the light.

Paul was pretty clear in the book of Romans. "Put aside the lusts of the flesh and put away the old man."

You have a choice to sin or not. Please never forget that.

#9 – MINISTER WHEN ASKED

I have mentioned this already, but want to include it in the list again for posterity. Make sure they ask for help first. This follows on perfectly. They must open their mouth and ask for help first. Sure, you can drop a few hints and say, "That must be tough. If you need any help, I am there for you."

However, after that, you must back off and wait for them to ask for help. Until they ask for help, everything you share and minister is just going to bounce off the wall and it is not going to touch them. You are just going to exhaust yourself. Give yourself a break.

#10 – DO NOT LAY HANDS SUDDENLY

Don't lay hands suddenly or feel compelled to lay hands and minister. The Word is clear about that. It says, "Lay hands on no man suddenly." Do not just go laying hands on people and say, "Let me pray for you."

We, prophets, get a little excited. I remember when I was first placed in prophetic office. I was so happy about being in office. I prophesied over everyone and wanted to pray for everyone because it was so exciting.

However, we need to grow up a bit and use a little bit of wisdom. Do not just go around laying hands on people. You do not know what is in their heart or what sin is there. Get revelation, take it easy, and wait for the Lord.

There have been times that people have come to me and said, "Please pray for me."

I had to say to them, "No. You are not ready yet."

"Please pray for me. Things are so tough."

"No. You are not ready yet. You are sorry for the consequences. You are not sorry for your sin. If I lay hands on you and pray for you right now, I am going to get a backlash because you do not mean business with God."

They just want me to take the circumstances away. They want to pray that everything goes away, but they do not want to look at their responsibility. They want to pray that their sickness goes away, their relationship comes right, and that their finances come in.

However, there is no mention that they are responsible. There is no mention that they have sinned and have been bitter. They leave out the important fact that they have been selfish and treated their spouse badly, which has resulted in the marital break up!

They have not realized that they need to change. They just want me to take a magic wand and make it go away. Do not fall into that trap. Don't lay hands suddenly on anyone.

#11 – THE DEMON WILL STILL BE THERE TOMORROW!

You are going to find out if someone means business when you put on the screws and say, "Let's look at your sin." Right there between the word "sin" and the period, you are going to find out if they mean business or not.

If they really mean business, they are going to at least follow through and listen. That is why you have to use wisdom and know when to talk and when to shut up. Learn to flow in the spirit and hear the Holy Spirit.

Do not just pounce on people, lay hands on them, hammer them and tell them to repent, and do your prophetic thing. Take it easy. The Lord will still be there tomorrow and so will that demon.

Sometimes we rush it before the person is ready. I know that it sounds pretty mean to say, "the demon will still be there tomorrow." But it is so true! Rather wait until they are ready and have success, than be a fool and "rush in" and get a backlash!

Deal with it in wisdom and you will only have to deal with it once.

FINAL POINTS TO REMEMBER

1. It is about the Person

I am going to end now with a few points for you to remember. Remember that the key to deliverance is not the demon, but the person.

Do not look at them and see demons. Look at them and see the compassion that Christ has for them. When you can do that, you can lead them to victory.

2. Tell a demon that is manifesting to be quiet.

3. Counsel by the Word

Did you notice, as I was sharing through this whole lecture, how often I used the Word? It cuts like a sword, doesn't it? It is one thing to say, "I think this" and a whole different thing to say, "The Word of God says."

It carries weight and power. When you counsel, especially when dealing with people's sin, you better know the Word.

4. Do not stop until you get victory.

If that person means business, follow through. At the beginning, it may take some time because you are feeling your way around, but you will learn how to sense in the spirit. Follow through until you get victory.

5.   **Use your prophetic authority**

Use visions, Urim and Thummim, and most importantly, use the Word because it is a double-edged sword.

PEARS –
DECEPTION WATCHLIST

CHAPTER 06 – PEARS – DECEPTION WATCHLIST

Nobody likes the thought of getting into deception. Deception for the prophet is like kryptonite to superman. You want to be as far from it as possible.

For many, as you start flowing in the gifts, you ask the question, "Am I going to get into deception? I am afraid to get into deception."

Just like people fear demons and avoid spiritual warfare, so also does the prophet fear deception and tries to veer from it. Even to the point of ignoring it and pretending that it could "never happen to you."

"If I leave the devil alone then he will leave me alone." I already blew that idea right out of the water in *Prophetic Warrior*.

Let's press the point.

"If I do not think about deception, I will not get into deception." With that kind of thinking – you are already in deception. So you might as well face it now and deal with it!

KEY PRINCIPLE

The most crippling aspect of
deception is the fear of it and not
the failure itself.

Think about that for a moment.

SATAN'S COUNTER INSURGENCE

When the enemy has tried all he can to discourage you
and has failed, he pulls out a weapon you do not
expect. You expect the roaring lion. You expect him to
pounce you from the shadows.

In fact, you are so adept at handling your sword in the
battlefield that you do not expect the poison-tipped
dagger jabbed into your ribs from behind.

That dagger has a name – Deception!

You step onto the battlefield expecting the battle lines,
but instead, you are met with silence. As you look
through the mist, you do not see the angel of light
standing behind you.

It is the thing you have feared the most. A sneak attack
from the mist. Prophet of God, there is a way to reveal
the work of the enemy. I have showed you what he
looks like from every angle. You have seen his structure
and his obvious attempts to destroy the church.

However, tell me something. What is a greater danger? The enemy storming your gates from without, or the spy that is within, subverting every plan of the King?

There is one sure way that satan can win this battle and it is not by force. It is by turning you against the Kingdom that you serve. Now if you are not aware of the fact that you can be turned, or are too arrogant to arm yourself for this attack, your heart will be pierced and before you know it, you will find yourself turning on the ones that you love.

That is the worse case scenario. You do not need to get to that point. You have learned to use your sword. Now it is time to dust off your shield and to guard your heart against this subversive work of the enemy.

Pick Up Your Shield

Now deception might feel like a huge mountain looming in front of you. Perhaps a mountain you wish you could go around. However, I have come to tell you that deception will happen.

Not only has it and will it happen again, but it is also a vital part of your training. We need it, if for nothing else than to remind us of how human we are.

Essential Armor for Counter Insurgence

In the next couple chapters, I am going to help you to identify deception and teach you how to avoid it. Unfortunately, it is one of those things in life that you can only understand when you have lived it for yourself.

I watch my children growing up and they have such big ideas of what they are going to do when they grow up. They have so many plans and visions. You can only look at them and smile.

Having been on the other side of the fence, you know what they are in for and you know that there is no way around some of the hardships that they will face.

They have to grow up and experience heartbreak and opposition in life. It is the only way that they will learn how to overcome it.

How else will they grow? If we were born with the knowledge of everything, then we would never grow.

> ### KEY PRINCIPLE
>
> Facing prophetic deception is the definitive transition between prophetic ministry and prophetic office.

In the next book in this series, the *Prophetic Key*, you will make the transition to office.

There is just one step to take before you get there. Now I know you are weary. You have been really pushing through! You have faced death to the flesh. You have buffeted your flesh and trained hard for spiritual warfare.

You have educated your mind and learned to flow in the spirit. Do you even realize how far that you have come?

Be that as it may, it is at this very step that I have seen so many trip... right before the finish line!

The Lord has been preparing you for this moment. He has been enabling you to handle it. The question is... are you going to give up now?

Are you going to take all the training that you have been through and walk away, just because of the flesh and deception? You paid the price! You pushed through. You are armed. You are dangerous.

After all is said and done, will you turn your sword on yourself and allow the enemy to win this battle? No, the final phase of your training beckons you to engage.

You are armed. You are ready. You know how to die. Now the question is... do you know how to face deception with grace?

Sorry, there is no shortcut on this one. There is only one way that you are going to make it to prophetic office and that is this big block called prophetic deception.

Until you have faced it and overcome it, you are not getting to office because there are some things that you need to learn.

WHY THE DECEPTION PHASE IS ESSENTIAL

> ### KEY PRINCIPLE
>
> The main point of why the deception phase is needed, is that you need to learn that it is not your ability to hear that makes you a prophet. It is God's ability to get through to you that enables you to hear.

We, prophets, become a bit filled with pride, because we can hear the Lord better than others can. We journal, we get visions, dreams and prophetic words, and when the Lord grows silent, what is your first reaction?

"Have I done something wrong? God is mad at me. I failed."

You start to think that this prophetic walk, your ability to hear God, is all about you and your ability to get into the spirit.

IT IS DEPENDENT ON HIM

> *2 Peter 1:21 for prophecy never came by the will of man, but holy men of God spoke as they were moved by the Holy Spirit.*

Peter tells us here that, "No prophetic word or revelation was given that man made up so that he could boast. It was given by the Holy Spirit."

Revelation is dependent on Him. It is not because you will, want, or need a word that you get one. It is because God wants to give one to you.

However, you forget that. You start becoming so comfortable and puffed up that you think it is up to you. You start thinking that you need to pray more, believe more, fast more and read the Word more to hear His voice better.

These things sure help, but at the end of the day, if He is not speaking, then He is not speaking.

It is up to Him to give you revelation and you forget that. You can be sure that a rude wake up call is on its way.

All you need now, is a nice trip down the road of prophetic deception to wake you up.

Trust me, this is a lesson that you will never forget. It is not up to you to hear the voice of God that sets you apart as a prophet. It is His ability and His choice to speak to you that makes you that prophet.

Colette Toach

Romans 11:29 For the gifts and the calling of God are irrevocable.

Do you know what is even more humbling? You can be in the midst of a sinful rampage and God will give you a word to minister to someone.

You can feel that you have lost all of your sanctification and like the biggest backslider in this world. Through all that garbage and trash… He will speak to you and give you a word and a revelation.

Why? Because the gifts are without repentance. They do not depend on you. The Lord requires faith and he will use Balaam or a donkey to speak if the person who needs to hear that word has faith. Have you ever wondered how someone who has clear sin in their life can still be used so mightily of the Lord?

It is because the gifts of God are just that… a gift. A gift that has only one prerequisite – faith! Sure, our righteousness ensures that we do not give the enemy license and impart a couple of viruses when we minister. If you keep blocking your ears to the Lord, then His voice will dim.

However even in such a state, if someone is praying in faith, God will throw you to the ground and talk to you, just like He did to Paul!

KEY PRINCIPLE

> You will realize that it is not because of your righteousness that He speaks, but it is because of His righteousness and holiness that He speaks.

There is no greater way to experience the grace of the Lord than to fall flat on your face in prophetic deception and for Him to pick you up and still use you, in spite of yourself, your sin and failure.

It is very humbling and also necessary to bring you to a place of humility where you walk before the Lord and know that you have this call because of Him.

TO IDENTIFY THE DIFFERENT VOICES

Another very important part of this process is so that you will finally come to understand the difference between the voice of your mind, the voice of the enemy, and the voice of the Lord.

Only when you have come to experience this for yourself, do you really know what the enemy sounds like. It is such a benefit because when others are in deception and you hear them, you will say, "I know that voice. That voice led me down the wrong road more than once before."

So now... there is no way around this one. You have to live it. So, brace yourself for it and deal with it.

I will give you this one little cheat though to prepare yourself... it will come when you least expect it.

You cannot plan for something called prophetic deception. That is why it is called... deception. If you knew that you were about to go into deception – it would not exactly be "deception" now, would it?

The Lord will test you in His way and in His time and you will know whether you have failed or passed that test only once it is over.

Only then, you will say, "I really fell into that trap."

I can help you through it, and I can tell you why it is necessary, but there is no way that I can help you escape it.

My job right now, is to equip you for it and to remove the fear so that you are ready to embrace it when it does come. Isn't that like all military training? The sergeant major can drill the troops. He can show them pictures, and even arrange mock drills.

All of these might equip the troops for battle, but there is nothing like engaging in actual warfare to prepare you. Nothing can prepare you for the emotional and physical stress you go through. You can understand it as much as you like, but as the saying goes, "There's nothing to it, but to do it!"

So yes, I am your sergeant major right now. I am drilling you and pushing you to do 10 more pushups. I am going to equip you, so that when you face it, what you have put into your spirit and mind will return to you in the heat of battle.

The moment you feel the poison-tipped dagger of the enemy pierce your side, the training and knowledge you have gained will rise up from deep within and you will know what to do. So do not skip this step. Study. Become equipped, and then… stand ready.

How the Process Begins

So, how does this process begin? If you have already gone through this, then you will understand. If you have not, then you are going to listen to these points and think, "I must remember that."

I promise that you will only remember after you have gone through it. Then, you will say, "I should have known that."

Now, us prophets, we run towards the cross. Death and travail? Bring it on! Deception… not so much.

None of us wake up saying, "Maybe today is the day that I will get into deception so that I can rise up."

No one is that stupid. Well I know that I am not that stupid! So that is why near the end of your prophetic training, you start to become confident. You may have started out unsure of your calling and anointing.

When you go through the training process, you are crushed down, built up, crushed down and built up.

However, towards the end, you start flowing in the gifts and you begin to "get it."

You start to think, "I am getting to the place where I know what God has called me to be. I am at the place where I see myself rising up into office. Actually, I am probably at the place now where I know as much as my leaders and mentors do.

I have understood the teaching on mentorship, and I think that I am around the place where I am at an equal footing from my mentor and I have received everything from them that I can. I am about at that level."

ENTER... GEHAZI

Do you know what that is like? It is like Elisha and Gehazi in 2 Kings 5. When the Naaman came and he asked to be healed, Elisha said, "Go and wash seven times in the River Jordan."

He does it and is healed. He returns to Elisha and says, "Thank you. I am healed and blessed. Let me give you some clothes and this money."

Elisha says, "I do not want it. I do not want to touch it."

Of course he did not want to touch it because it was contaminated. Remember what I said about contaminated objects? The leprosy crippling that man did not come about just because he ate bad sushi! He had been bowing down to idols!

He had offered his body up to the enemy and had been contaminated from head to toe. (Everything you learned in the first chapter should be making more sense to you.)

Elisha did not want anything to do with it.

However, Gehazi thought, "Elisha does not really know any better. I have been with him for a while now and I think I can teach him a thing or two here."

So he ran after Naaman and took the money and clothing from him. What happened to Gehazi? He ends up with the same leprosy that Naaman had.

This graphic illustration is for your benefit, because this is exactly what will happen to you.

GOD SETS YOU UP

You will come to a place where you have the temptation to do things your way. The Lord will open the way where you will have the freedom to make a choice.

You will have this mentor on your back who has always put pressure on you saying, "Die to your flesh. Let go of your sin."

Then, you start becoming a bit arrogant and think that you alone are responsible for your prophetic calling.

You say, "It is time that I get my own conviction and that I decide the road that I am going to walk. I feel according to the Word that I have the right to choose.

I think that right now, although my mentor has been good and although he has been there with me along the way and helped me, I am at the point where I am starting to see things that he is not."

Careful Gehazi... you are running head long into that deception, hook, line and sinker. Then, you cannot understand why you end up in bondage and everything goes wrong.

It leads you into rebellion and even though the opening seems to be of God, it pushes you beyond what God has intended. It warps what God has given you. The worst part is that you come out from the authority that you are under. In that moment, it feels like all Hell breaks loose.

SHOCKWAVES

Everything starts going wrong. Suddenly, your spirit feels blocked, curses are rampant, you are in conflict with everybody, you are fighting and you are feeling the conflict in your own spirit and you do not know why.

You think, "It is because of that mentor!"

You say, "They are putting so much pressure on me all the time. They do not understand what I am going through right now. I know that they are used of God and can hear from God, but right now I need to hear from God for myself, because I do not believe they are hearing from God anymore."

They could hear from God when they called you to mentorship, but now they cannot hear from God when it comes to the end of your training?

That should be a warning sign.

Remember what I said over and over again in the *Prophetic Boot Camp* book?

"I never said it has to be fair."

You know what? Perhaps your assessment is even correct, but what is the spirit behind your motivation? Is God calling you to submit, not because it is right, but simply because you need to learn to submit?

You have in you a spirit of rebellion, independence, and control. You want to be in charge. It is not about who is right and who is wrong. Can you not see that it is about what God wants?

The minute you start finding yourself saying, "I think this. You must understand me. This is about my call..." you need to be careful.

I hear a whole lot of "me, myself, and I" in that rampage of yours. So tell me prophet... What did God say?

"I do not feel very comfortable with this situation. Therefore, I do not believe that it is of God and therefore I am going my own way."

Hello Gehazi, you just fell for satan's trap. Unfortunately, with tests like that, you only recognize them when it is too late and you have already fallen. That is what is so devastating about prophetic deception.

NOTHING HALF-HEARTED FOR THE PROPHET

You do not see it coming. You do not just slip and fall into it. You run, leap and give one hundred percent as you hit that wall good and solid. If there is one thing us prophets can do... it's mess up with style!

If we are going to get into deception and mess up, then we are going to make a show of it. You are going to open your big, mouth and say what you think and you are going to be arrogant, proud, and strong.

You are going to hit that wall and it has to be that way. It is only the tests that you fail so gloriously that will wake and shake you up and make you see what God is trying to teach you.

DECEPTION WATCH LIST - PEARS

Be that as it may, I am still going to give you a neat little list to help you navigate through this phase properly. Now it is quite likely that you will identify with each of these points, only once you have fallen for them.

The good news is, that if you can learn each one of them, you only need fail once. No need to be a glutton for punishment! One prophetic deception is good enough for any prophet-in-training. Do not be a hog now and overindulge on it!

So study and make note of these points. Not only will they ensure that you are protected from all future attacks of deception, but it will help you identify it in others as well.

I sure hope that you face it in others, because then you will see just exactly what your poor mentor had to go through with you. There is nothing quite like having that same nasty poison spewed all over you, to suddenly feel compassion for the last guy you dumped on!

Very soon these principles will become your own, but they are not yours yet. So do not just read these points. Memorize and study them until they become your own.

To help you out, I have chosen a nice acronym for you to use. Like fruit? Then you are going to love PEARS – a quick way to avoid deception! Using this word tickles me, because Eve ate fruit to sin, but now you can use it to reverse that effect!

1. PUSHED TO DO SOMETHING NOW (PUSHINESS)

The first warning that deception is knocking at your door, is that you feel pushed to act on revelation immediately. In fact, it is so urgent that if you do not do it right now... people will die!

Wait on that one. Wait on that revelation. If that feeling goes away, it is quite likely that your revelation was not of the Lord.

Yet, if in time, God gives confirmation, then you can step out cautiously. Any time that you are pushed and feel like you must speak now, do the opposite. Wait.

2. WATCH OUT FOR INTENSE EMOTION (EMOTIONAL)

Now I am not talking just about negative emotions here. You can be excited and compelled and feel more positive than you have ever felt in your life. In fact, the emotion is so strong that you revert to point 1... you get pushy!

When you feel that, wait.

Why? It is because the Holy Spirit is gentle. He is a dove. He nudges you. He woos you. He does not hammer you over the head and say, "Do it now!"

That is not His style. You should know that by now. If you are doing something and a revelation comes out of nowhere accompanied by uncontrollable emotion... stop.

You get so caught up in your excitement about your revelation, that you want to jump up and tell the world. You end up imposing and pushing that revelation on the poor unsuspecting soul that crosses your path.

Just because it felt great does not mean that it was of God. Wait. The Lord does not speak that way. You should know that by now.

Think about when you are ministering and you get a revelation. Sometimes you are not even sure that it is His voice because it is so gentle, He nudges. He whispers in your ear.

He is a gentleman. He does not hit you with a steam roller.

3. WATCH OUT FOR ARROGANCE

You are in a very dangerous place when you begin to hear yourself boasting, "I got this revelation from God." From there you go on to impress everyone with the color and magnificence of your vision. Others who cannot hear God in this way say, "Ooooh! Aaaah! You are so amazing!"

It makes you look so good and you go around saying, "I saw this vision. I had this experience."

Everyone does not look at you and say, "Wow. God is so good." They say, "Wow. You are so amazing."

It is not difficult to see it in others too. It is scary. They will say, "What a great man of God. He must be so close to God."

John the Baptist said, "Let me decrease that He may increase." If you are increasing and the Lord is decreasing, there is a problem here.

If they are talking about how great you are instead of how great God is, we have a problem. Watch out for those revelations and keep them to yourself. Unless they are really going to minister to someone, keep them to yourself, put them past your mentor. Let God confirm.

There are times that my husband tells me the most intimate and romantic things. Things that make my knees weak. How crass would I be to step out of our bedroom and repeat everything he said to the whole world, just so that they could say, "Wow! You are such a lucky wife!"

If I shared those intimate moments, just to brag, it stains the beauty of the moment. It is the same with the revelation that God gives to you. There are things that He shares during your times of intercession that are just for you. "Sweet nothings" to tell you how precious you are to Him.

Do not cheapen them, by using them to make yourself look amazing. Not only is it insulting to Jesus, but if all you want are "super duper" revelations, you can be sure that the enemy has plenty of those to give you.

That angel of light is standing behind you. His dagger in hand, ready to strike your heart. When he does, make sure that your heart is resting securely in the love of Jesus and not in the love of the recognition of man.

4. Rebellion Against Authority (Rebellion)

"I am sick of you telling me what to do. It is time that I decide for myself what to believe here."

"I know that God has put you in my life and I know that you are my leader, but..."

Be careful. It is not about who is right or wrong. It is about what God wants. Bite your tongue. Hold the words and wait. You are not in prophetic office yet! If the Lord put you under a mentor to take you through the entire training process, why would He take you out to appoint you to office?

Until you are in prophetic office, stay where God has sent you! If He has lead you to receive, then receive until you reach the goal. Has God told you to remain at your church and submit to a pastor? Has He told you to submit to your husband?

If so, then why would He contradict Himself? The reality is that you know God has put you there, but they are now telling you things that you do not want to hear.

5. DON'T SEEK REVELATION OUT (SEEKING)

With a church that is so hyped over each new revelation, it does not take much to get caught up in the wave. Watch out for trying to seek out new revelation.

With endless books being written about angels, demons, and the end times, it does not take a lot to make you feel like a second rate prophet. As if being a prophet is all about the fantastic revelations of the spirit.

Here is the thing – the realm of the spirit is an amazing place. For the longest time during my prophetic training, the Lord Jesus showed me so many wonderful things.

I grew so much as a believer. I came to know Jesus face-to-face. I experienced amazing things, and it was through these experiences that I matured. However, here is the reality. I could not remain there.

All my great experiences did nothing to change a single person. Sure, I could share about the times I had with the Lord, and it might have inspired someone – but hearing my stories did not draw them into a face-to-face relationship with Jesus.

I had to teach them to do it for themselves. I had to lead them into experiencing Jesus for themselves. All the experiences and revelations in the world did nothing but tickle their ears. It is only an applied revelation that brings real change.

What use is it to share all my super duper experiences in the Throne Room, unless it is to show you how to get there yourself? So if you are not having these experiences, then you are just where God needs you to be – changing lives!

If you are having these experiences, then that is great – but you cannot live there. There comes a time when you have to step out of your world and into the reality, where the Church is living!

The worst mistake that you can make is to seek out such experiences. To seek out angels, demons, and a new revelation. You will experience the realm of the spirit, alright, but which realm will you find yourself caught in?

Do not find yourself on the receiving end of this passage,

> *Colossians 2:18 Let no one cheat you of your reward, taking delight in false humility and worship of angels, intruding into those things which he has not seen, vainly puffed up by his fleshly mind,*

We do not worship angels – we worship Christ. We are not invited into a face to face relationship with angels, but with Jesus. Do not seek out revelation. Do not seek out angels. Seek out Christ and trust me... revelation follows naturally!

PEARS - REVIEW

Have you got your PEARS straight? Keep them in mind always to guard yourself against deception. This will indeed become a shield that will protect you from the arrows of the enemy.

Memorize each point and when you fall prey to the work of the enemy, recall this acronym and remember what tripped you up. Sure, you are a prophet, you might stumble and fall, but it does not mean you have to stay down.

Watch out devil, cause this prophet might have stumbled over his own feet, but he will rise up again with sword in hand and with a very bad temper – ready to take you out!

> **P** – Pushiness
>
> **E** – Emotional
>
> **A** – Arrogance
>
> **R** – Rebellion
>
> **S** – Seeking Revelation

WATCH YOUR TONE!

CHAPTER 07 – WATCH YOUR TONE!

Nothing counts more than being able to have your voice heard above the noise. Try sitting at the dinner table at one of our ministry centers and you will know what I am talking about.

Everyone talks at once, trying to get their idea or joke across. Trying to make a point at the crescendo of the cacophony is a skill in itself. There is a way through it though. All that needs to happen is that my husband, Craig, needs to speak up.

They know his voice. It booms through the air and everyone dies down in their conversation to hear what "Dad" has to say. They know the familiar resonance of his voice along with that particular "tone" he uses when he means business. Nothing can shut a room up quicker!

This perhaps is a naturalistic illustration, but do you know what voice counts in your spiritual life? Are you well able to hear the voice of your heavenly Father through the crescendo of cacophony in your life? Do your ears prick up to that familiar tone that He uses when He calls your name?

In the *Prophetic Functions* book, you learned to hear the voice of the Lord, but I have another way for you to know what is God, and what is not.

When you can learn which voice does not belong to the Lord, the truth of His words will echo through your uncertainty.

You know how to hear His voice, so how about you begin identifying which voice does not belong to Him? It is perhaps a different way of looking at it, but is extremely vital for this phase of your training.

WATCH THAT TONE!

There is a reason that satan is called an angel of light! He can imitate revelations and the voice of God. Although he really does try to "throw his voice" across the battlefield in an attempt to trick you, there are some things that are just obvious.

For the life of him, satan just cannot get that "tone" right. There is just a certain tone in a parent's voice when they mean business. I bet that you can hear the voice of your mother telling you it is time to come home from play.

You can hear your father's "tone" telling what was not acceptable in the house. It would not matter what situation you were in - you can spot that "tone" from a mile away!

Well it is the same for the Lord. There is an emotion and "tone" in His voice that sets Him apart.

> **KEY PRINCIPLE**
>
> No matter how much the enemy tries to imitate the Lord, he has a tone of his own that is quite distinctive.

Well that is what I want to show you here. In fact, once you read these simple points below, the penny will drop.

You will remember times when you heard the voice of the enemy and thought it was the Lord. Then you will recognize times when you were so pumped about this great "revelation" only to discover that it was just your own mind doing all the talking!

THE VOICE OF THE ENEMY

1. LOUD AND PUSHY

The enemy has two faces. The one is a roaring lion and the second is an angel of light. His first modus operandi is to push you beyond what God intends. A revelation from him will make you feel that you have to take action immediately!

You will feel that if you do not take action "right now" that you will fail the Lord and everyone around you. You feel that if you do not do something, that all will be lost. Your faith is shifted to your own works instead of the Lord's ability to intervene.

2. SELF-JUSTIFIED

When the enemy cannot get you to push beyond what God intends, He will seek to comfort you. He will allow you to think, "It is alright. You did not do anything wrong. It was everyone else that was out of line. You are justified to hold onto your anger and frustration."

His voice justifies your sin with excuses and reasoning. His voice will say, "Well how could anyone judge you from making that decision? Look at the hard time you faced!" His voice subverts the work of the cross. Instead of leading you to the cross towards repentance, it will justify your sin and give you a "way to escape" from your failure. An escape that will not lead to the cross, but to your destruction, giving him just the open door he wanted in your life.

3. OBTRUSIVE

Satan is really a rude type! He will push into a conversation or a quiet time and demand that you take an action or receive a revelation. The Lord Jesus always woos and invites. He does not impose His will.

He draws you into your prayer closet – He does not dump it on you! The Holy Spirit will wake you in the night and you will feel a gentle tug to go into His presence. The enemy will impose a dream or revelation on you that will push you to your bed and take over your mind!

He will give revelations that impose and that you cannot control. He will override your senses and force you to listen to him. The Lord Jesus is the Good Shepherd who leads, the enemy is the butcher driving from behind.

4. QUESTIONS GOD'S WORD

When tricking a prophet, the enemy knows better than to give you a revelation that contradicts the Word completely. Especially if you are strong in the Word! Rather, he will say to you as he did to Eve, "Did God say...?"

God will give you a promise through the Spirit or the Word and you will cling to it. However, as time passes the thoughts start to come to your mind, "Did God really say...?"

When tough times come and your promise is not coming to pass, the voice gets louder. The more you dwell on it, the more it begins to override the word that God gave to you.

Cling to the Scriptures. Dwell on the promises you know to be true. The enemy is the father of lies, so if he is telling you something, then you can count on the opposite being true! Has he questioned that promise? Well then you can rest assured that it is going to come to pass!

Has his voice in your mind questioned your call? Well then you can stand in the truth of God's promise of its surety! In trying to deceive, satan only confirms what God has said, because no true word can come from his mouth.

5. FEAR, GUILT, SELF-PROMOTION

Fear steals faith. Guilt and self-promotion destroy hope and love. You already know that every word should have faith, hope and love. How about we switch it up and look at what every revelation should *not* have?

You know that your sword should be sharp and your breastplate strapped securely to your chest. However, what your sword should not have is rust or a dent! Your breastplate should not be broken and your helmet scuffed up!

Let's get rid of what contaminates your weapons of warfare. Fear, guilt and self-promotion damage your armor, making you less effective.

When you hear a voice that causes you to fear, losing your sound mind, this is not of the Lord. This is the voice of the enemy trying to rattle you! When fear grips you to the point of being too afraid to open up your mouth to speak, you can be sure something is very wrong!

God is not going to give you a revelation and then make you too afraid to speak it! Now on the other hand, if you share a word that brings gripping fear to the hearer – take caution! This was not the voice of the Lord Jesus at all.

The same is true of guilt and condemnation. Jesus told us all that He did not come to judge the world, but to save it! The Word stands as the only true judge! A word that causes someone to come under the "sorrow of the world" is not a word from God.

Then finally, self-promotion. This is a biggie, but one that is quite rampant in the church. It is so unfortunate, because these words take the eyes of God's people off the cross and onto the speaker of that revelation.

When someone has to give a word to "prove that he is a prophet" he has changed sides to deliver that revelation! Why on earth do I need to prove that I am prophet?

I have a sword, shield, and the Lord knows, I can use it. Hello?! Want to know if I am a prophet, just try messing with God's people and you will find out soon enough. Why should I waste my time trying to prove myself to you?

I would rather use all my faith, hope, and love proving the love and grace of Christ. His position and work in this world is far greater than mine. I am just the vessel. It would be like a jar of wine saying, "Check me out! Ain't I the coolest wine jar you ever saw?"

What use would that jar be, without the wine it contains? Without any wine to pour out, would that jar even find its way to the banqueting table? So why should we (the jarheads) boast about something we do not own?

Our only boast? God decided to pour His wine into us and set us on the table, so that we might be poured out. Its not the jar that must be proved, but the wine. Any revelation that is for the sole purpose of proving your call and yourself, is the enemy leading you astray.

Are you beginning to see this in others also? The flesh is nasty! Let us not give satan a foothold. I tell you what, why don't we just hike on back to Golgotha, you and I, and find our resting place there again? That is surely when the wine pours out the most!

THE VOICE OF YOUR MIND

Identifying the voice of the enemy is actually easier than the voice of your own mind. Because the Holy Spirit is indwelling, when you journal, His voice often sounds like your own.

That is why it is tricky sometimes to determine if a revelation you got was God's idea or just a really good one you just came up with!

The good news is, that although the logic of your mind can lead you astray, if you stay submitted to the Lord, the worst you can do is give really bad advice.

I will talk a bit on the different kinds of deception shortly, but for now try to think back on times where the voice you heard had the "tone" of your mind.

1. Logical

The first sign that the voice you are hearing is just your own mind, emotions and will, is that it will be logical. You will think that you are sharing such great ideas and advice... and perhaps you are. The thing is, does that mean it is revelation?

There is nothing wrong with sharing the obvious with people, but do not call it revelation. Just because you are good at using illustrations to share a point, does not mean you got revelation. It just means that you understand how things work.

Many prophets make the mistake of using their personality power to make a point, calling it revelation. No, let us put that right where it belongs. You just shared really good advice and ideas.

It came from your own mind – not from God's. How do you know that? Well because the word "revelation" says it all. Revelation reveals something to you that you did not know before.

Do not assume that just because you have some life experience and know a few principles that what you share is revelation. Did you really hear from God? Was the revelation you received fresh, or is it the logical conclusion that anyone else could have received?

If someone else, who is a good leader, could share your same ideas, then are you still sure that you got revelation? No, you are just well studied. You will know a true revelation when it comes. It will be something you did not think of before! In fact, many times, that revelation will cut across what you thought it would be.

You would have determined that the person should go right, but the revelation indicates that they should go left!

2. EMOTION DRIVEN

Here is another good tip. If you are too emotionally engaged in the revelation, you might want to step back a little. Are you sharing revelation or just your own hobby horse? A good way to find out is to have someone reject that word!

Did you take it personally? So again – was the word the Lord's or your own? If it was the Lord's what are you getting so offended about?

> *KEY PRINCIPLE*
>
> If you are taking rejection personally, then it might be a good time to determine if your revelation is of the Lord, or just your idea.

How can you take ownership of a true revelation? If it never originated with you, then you cannot claim ownership, can you? So why be offended if it is not received? You might be discouraged for the person's sake, but you should not feel personally offended!

Keep taking on personal offense? It might be a good time to determine if the word was the Lord's or your own.

3. YOUR OWN TEMPLATES AND BURDENS

If you find yourself giving revelations that center around your own archetype, templates, and habits in life, you might want to wait on that one! It goes back to the point where I said, "If it is logical, watch out for that!"

You start saying things like, "The Lord wants you to worship in this way." In a way that just so happens to be the way that you worship! You start giving prophetic words that try to convince others of a doctrine that you are firm on.

Are you in deception? Not yet, but you are heading there pretty fast if you keep imposing your own burdens on others.

More than once I have heard an evangelist prophecy that everyone should "win the lost." True revelation, or just the voice of their own mind echoing their personal ministry burden?

Now it is not bad to share a word like that, but then do not say, "Thus saith the Lord!" Rather say, "Thus saith the prophet!"

If you share words that try to manipulate others to think like you do, or to share your ministry burden, you are just hearing what you want to hear. Your revelation is obvious and way too close to home. No wonder the Lord delights in sending prophets out of their comfort zones! That way, you are less likely to remain in your hobby horse!

THE VOICE OF GOD

You certainly know what the voice of the Lord is like. However, take a moment now to contrast it to what you just learned about the voice of the enemy and your own mind. When you do that, the voice of the Lord will become clearer than ever before!

1. DRAWS YOU TO CHRIST

> *John 16:13 However, when He, the Spirit of truth, has come, He will guide you into all truth; for He will not speak on His own authority, but whatever He hears He will speak; and He will tell you things to come.*
> *14 He will glorify Me, for He will take of what is Mine and declare it to you.*

I love this passage! Here Jesus tells us that the Holy Spirit will not speak of Himself, but will always point to

Christ! The voice of God always glorifies Jesus. It draws us closer into the embrace of our Bridegroom.

Any revelation that forces a wedge between you and the love of Jesus is not the Lord. Any tradition of man or any new doctrine that separates you from Jesus is not the voice of the Lord. The Holy Spirit cannot help Himself... He will always draw you closer to Christ.

If that means separating you from sin, so be it! If it means warning you, so be it! Whether it is a tender, or strong word, the result will always be the same – you will take a step closer to Jesus.

2. FAITH, HOPE AND LOVE

You should know this one by now! A word from the Lord will always motivate your faith, hope, and love. It will not puff up your flesh, or condone your sin. Rather it will motivate you towards the cross and make you ready to run your race unhindered by any weight!

3. CONFIRMS AND WITNESSES

A word from the Lord will witness in your spirit and confirm what you have already heard. Be cautious of revelations that come out of the blue and have nothing to do with what you have been praying for, or have already heard from the Lord.

Any word you share should confirm what God has already been telling that person. God will not contradict Himself.

4. Brings Forth Fruit to Repentance

How powerful! A true word from the Lord will bring you to your knees. There is nothing quite like a tender word from Jesus to make the blackness of my heart stand out. When God speaks, our human heart hungers.

We hunger for the embrace of our Father. Our spirits cry out for His touch and any word from His mouth will echo over the noise and make us want to run into His arms. We will gladly strip off any bondage that is holding us back.

5. Confirms His Word

The voice of God never contradicts itself. Revelation will always confirm His Word. It will piece together the bits and pieces that you did not understand from the Scriptures, making them alive! In fact, I would daresay that the revelation that the prophet gets, will take the the Scriptures and make them come alive.

Revelation from the Lord breathes life into the promises you have received and the Scriptures you have read. They take logos words and transform them into rhema!

Deception Types

Now before you panic because you gave someone good advice instead of true revelation, let's just understand deception a bit. Ok, so you were a bit overzealous and told someone that you feel God is going to give them a son and they gave birth to a daughter.

Yes, it might not have been smart to say, "I see you marrying a blonde" and they walked down the isle with a brunette! We all make mistakes and it is not going to be the last time that you let your mind do all the talking instead of the voice of God.

There are different forms of deception, and I would daresay that the first category falls more into "misconception" than deception! Where you confuse revelation with a good idea. There will be times when you will give advice instead of revelation.

There will be times when you will impose your ministry burden instead of truly hearing from God. For the most part, you can shake yourself free of this. Where you need to be careful, is when you start moving into the realm of mixing the truth that God is giving you with the lie of the enemy.

This is where the waters become muddied and the first step towards full blown deception. So consider the three categories of deception, which are:

1. **Misconception**
2. **Contamination**
3. **Deception**

1ST CATEGORY: YOUR MIND - MISCONCEPTION

Like I already said, this is where you listen to your logical mind instead of taking time to really hear the voice of the Lord. In these situations, you really told the person what you thought and not what God said!

This happens more often than you realize. Now there is nothing wrong with giving advice (if someone asked for it) but then do not call it revelation.

Because you are a neat freak, do not go around giving people a word from God saying, "You need to clean your house!" If you cannot stand loud and pushy people do not go around telling churches that they need to, "Deal with loud and pushy people!"

Get your own opinions out of the way, so that the true word of God can shine through!

2ND CATEGORY: MIXED VOICES – CONTAMINATION

This is where things start getting messy. It is a situation where you get a true word from the Lord, but then it gets contaminated with something that is not of the Lord.

Either you add your own pre-conceived ideas (from your mind) to it, or the enemy takes your revelation and pushes it beyond what was intended.

I taught on this a bit in the *Way of Dreams and Visions* book if you want to go into more detail. The bottom line is that you got something real that became contaminated with either a push from the enemy or your flesh.

This happens when you have not been through enough training and you allow your pre-conceived ideas to influence your revelation.

This also takes place when you have a demonic bondage in your life that contaminates the word. Was the word of the Lord? Yes, it was! However, because you are bound by the enemy yourself, even the true word ends up yielding bad fruit. Why? Because the fruit in the prophet is bad!

> ### KEY PRINCIPLE
>
> Always remember – it is not about how great your revelation is, it is about the spirit that motivates that revelation.

Now is a good time for me to mention that this is where most of your testing will take place in the deception phase of your training. If you have any demonic bondages though, you can be sure that they will manifest as the third category.

3RD CATEGORY: SATAN'S PLAN - DECEPTION

Now where things get really dangerous is when the word received is outright deception. A word that originates with the enemy. It is not a word that he added to your original revelation. It is not even an idea gone wrong.

It is the kind of word that wakes you up in the middle of the night saying, "You have to share this now!" I am talking about the kind of word that drips with fear and leaves a spirit of heaviness and strife in its wake.

There are two keys for this form of deception, and you will find them mentioned in the Word as the angel of light, and a spirit of divination. These two are not just motivated by a bad attitude. They are false revelations. Words of satan. The very plan of the enemy to distract and tear down what God wants to do.

You are going to come into confrontation with both of these, so allow me to arm you against them. Identify them and be sure to root any of it out of your life.

ANGEL OF LIGHT

> *2 Corinthians 11:14 And no wonder! For Satan himself transforms himself into an angel of light. 15 Therefore it is no great thing if his ministers also transform themselves into ministers of righteousness, whose end will be according to their works.*

THE APPEARANCE OF RIGHTEOUSNESS

Just because a person appears righteous does not mean he produces the fruit of the spirit! In fact, it was those who were "super righteous" and looked down their noses at others that Paul was talking about in this scripture.

An angel of light comes across with strength and a sense of "knowing better." It causes the hearer to feel insecure as if what they heard from God is not good enough. What causes greater damage on a battlefield? A roaring lion or a general dressed in the same uniform as your own?

The angel of light is not a roaring lion. It is dressed in the same uniform as a righteous one. He speaks the same and walks the same. However, the tone is all wrong! It imposes and forces you to listen. In fact, you will feel a force coming at you demanding that you receive.

You will feel as if you are missing God if you do not listen. This fear will drive you to receiving its revelation. Since when did the Lord Jesus shed His blood to make us feel second rate?

When I dwell on His love, that love moves me even more. When I think of His blood, I am broken to the core and want to wrap my arms around His neck. I do not want to run from His presence, I want to run into it!

KEY PRINCIPLE

My calling and worth is confirmed at
the cross – not questioned.

CONFUSION AND STRIFE

A revelation that comes from an angel of light will
confuse the truth. What you thought was once true will
suddenly not make sense. There will be confusion in
the camp. Where before everyone was in unity, strife
will begin to surface.

Divisions and conflicts will suddenly rise up out of
nowhere. Solid teams will become frustrated with one
another. Families who stood firm in the storm will
begin to fight amongst themselves. Ministry teams will
start to separate and no longer share the same vision.
Each one will want to pull their way.

WORKS OF THE FLESH

An angel of light will distract a person from their true
direction and cause them to become distracted. They
will follow after things that promote the flesh and go
against what God has told them.

They will run after the "pot of gold at the end of the
rainbow" only to find that no gold exists. Strife and
vainglory will become rampant. They will strive
amongst themselves hungering after the things of the

flesh. Each will promote their own visions and what they want to see come to pass.

The motivation will no longer be about extending the Kingdom of God, but about "My vision" and "My desire" for God. "Me, Myself and I" will take the center stage – and why not? Can you think of any better way for the enemy to tear the church apart than from within?

DESTRUCTION AND THEFT FOLLOW

You can be sure that if the enemy is giving an order, it is not for the purpose of "equipping" and "building up" of the saints! His words will leave a trail of destruction and theft behind. Loss of money, car accidents and sickness follow the work of the enemy.

Think about it. You learned in the *Prophetic Warrior* what the structure of satan's kingdom looked like. He is looking for an open door in your life. Open up and receive a word from an angel of light and what more does he need from you?

You just shot an arrow on his behalf and gave him the license that he needed! So where did this angel of light come from?

DEALING WITH AN ANGEL OF LIGHT

I have shared a lot about how satan gains license, but I will share this with you. If you keep seeing a trail of destruction and broken ministries in your wake, it is time to step forward and pay attention.

Do you feel that you have an angel of light interfering with what God is trying to do in your life? Identify its entry point!

Is this generational? Did this begin after you received an impartation from someone? Perhaps you got into some strange doctrine at one time and ever since then, you have been receiving these "pushy" revelations that are starting to make you feel unsure.

Once you identify the open door, you know where to start repenting. I know that it seems like a big deal and no one wants to think that they fell prey to an angel of light, but it happens more than you know.

The important part is to be brave enough to face it. It is one thing to face the devil, it is another to face yourself!

I think that any prophet would sooner take on satan and every ruler demon in hell than to find themselves looking back at them on a battlefield. However, when you continue to receive revelation from an angel of light and cling to it, that is exactly what you are doing. You are making yourself, your own worse enemy!

KEY PRINCIPLE

> Be willing to face your own
> deception. If you cling to revelation
> from an angel of light, you are
> making yourself your own worst
> enemy.

There is no shame in admitting you were in deception.
The shame is in knowing it and not bringing it to the
cross. The shame is needing your revelations and
experiences more than you hunger for the simplicity of
Christ.

SPIRIT OF DIVINATION

> *Ezekiel 13:7 Have you not seen a futile vision,
> and have you not spoken false divination? You
> say, The Lord says,' but I have not spoken.
> 8 Therefore thus says the Lord God: Because
> you have spoken nonsense and envisioned lies,
> therefore I am indeed against you, says the Lord
> God.*

The "roaring lion" is the spirit of divination. Here is the
trickiest part of all – this is a revelation that often
comes to pass!

Either it leads someone in the opposite direction to
what God intends, or its dark revelation comes to pass
and grips people with fear.

If you read the two scriptures I picked out for this subject, you will see how the Lord also refers to it as witchcraft and compares it to someone that consults with a familiar spirit!

> *KEY PRINCIPLE*
>
> Just because a word comes to pass, does not necessarily mean it is from the Lord.

It lies primarily in the realm of New Age, psychics and Satanists. It is the essence of the voice of satan, deeming his bad will into the earth. It is a sad day when a prophet takes this voice on as their command and finds themselves fighting the war for the opposing army.

PSYCHICS VS. PROPHETS

> *Deuteronomy 18:10 There shall not be found among you anyone who makes his son or his daughter pass through the fire, or one who practices witchcraft, or a soothsayer, or one who interprets omens, or a sorcerer,*
> *11 or one who conjures spells, or a medium, or a spiritist, or one who calls up the dead.*

It is probably why I am so passionate about not allowing former "psychics" into any form of leadership position in the church until they have had complete deliverance. I have seen so many instances of "diviners" getting born again and simply using their "gift" for the Church instead of monetary gain.

The worst part? Many of the revelations come to pass. They see someone die in an accident and that person dies just so. They dream that something terrible happens and it happens.

Simply because it happens, people assume that their word is directly from God! So when the magicians also turned their staffs into serpents, in the time of Moses, was that a work of God?

In fact, they duplicated a number of the plagues, tricking Pharaoh into thinking that the God of Israel was no better than his own demons. Are we so different in the Church today?

If there is power in the spoken word of God, did you really think that a word from satan would be impotent? If satan's word goes out through the mouth of a willing vessel that truly believes in it, you can be sure it is going to do some damage. As a prophet it is not only your place to expose these double agents but to make sure that you are fighting on the right side too!

The fruit of the prophet and the Word is essential to identifying a spirit of divination. What was left in the wake of this revelation? Death, fear, and loss? Division, strife and confusion?

Or on the other hand, were they drawn closer to the Lord Jesus? Were you drawn to bow down and worship an angel or the Lord Jesus Christ? You will come across this often as a prophet, so take time to dwell on these points and to be aware of them.

You will encounter the spirit of divination more than once. When you do, make sure that you are armed with the truth!

9 WAYS TO AVOID DECEPTION

I have covered a number of points, but I do not want to end without some practical tips on how to get past this messy affair. Like I said before, you only need to make one of these mistakes once to never want to do it again.

One thing we all have in common is that we hunger for the presence of the Lord Jesus. We want to heal the broken hearted and are cut up when we see innocent sheep being dragged through the mud.

To imagine, for just one moment, that you were the cause of hurt or destruction is a death nail in itself. No true prophet of God ever wants to be the very thing he fights so hard against in the Church! So take note of these points and make them your own.

I might not be able to help you avoid the deception phase altogether, but I can certainly help you get out of it before you fall too deep and get past it as quickly as possible!

1. DON'T FLEECE THE LORD

Do you know the story of Gideon who put the fleece out? He said, "If the fleece is dry and the ground is wet, then I know that you are going to be with me as I fight for Israel."

Well that is what it means to put a fleece before the Lord. You will be walking in dangerous waters. Gideon did it once and never again. In my opinion, he was pushing it in the first place! When poor Moses tried to argue with God, he got some strong words back at him, not a neatly wrapped up fleece!

So when you say, "Lord, do this one thing, and then I will do what you asked me to."

"Lord if you give me a clear sign from heaven, then I will know that this word is from you."

Watch it prophet, you are walking on some shaky ground there.

The enemy has every opportunity to make that happen. Maybe it is of the Lord and maybe it is of the enemy, but you will never know now will you?

If you put a fleece before the Lord, you are asking for deception.

2. LISTEN SAFELY

When it comes to flowing in the gifts, learn to listen to the voice of the Lord in safety. Learn to listen for yourself first. Learn within your group, if you have a church where you meet to pray.

If you have a mentor, share your revelations with them. Practice in a safe environment first so that you can gain confidence.

When you are not sure of a revelation, go to your mentor, group, or the people that you have around you.

Say, "Hey, what do you think of this revelation?"

There is no shame in asking for help. The shame is in opening your big mouth and declaring to the whole world something that is way off beam – thus falling flat on your face.

That can end up being humiliating. So, do yourself a favor. You can look like a hotshot, if you are prepared to have some humility. First go to your mentor or spiritual leader.

Submit to them, listen to them, and then once you are confident, you can stand up and look good. People listening will not even know how much you had to go through to get to this point.

However, if you are going to really mess up, do yourself a favor and mess up in a safe environment. This is not for my benefit, or your leaders' benefit, but for your benefit.

If you are so full of pride that you are too afraid to reveal your mistakes to those that God has given you, then you can go out there and reveal your mistakes to everyone else, but you are going to regret it.

Use the opportunity that you have right now. Prophesy over yourself. Get visions for yourself. Start in your prayer closet and work your way from there.

3. SUBMIT YOUR REVELATIONS FOR VETTING

> *1 Corinthians 14:31 For you can all prophesy one by one, that all may learn and all may be encouraged.*
> *32 And the spirits of the prophets are subject to the prophets.*

You really want to do this when you get a clear revelation – especially if they are directional. Perhaps, the Lord gives you a revelation that says, "This person should move to another country."

Get some confirmation. In the mouths of two or three witnesses, let every word be established. Go to someone that you trust and that you know can hear the voice of God and get confirmation.

If you are married and your husband or wife are standing with you, even better. Go to them and ask them what they sense and feel. Do not just run off on a tangent all by yourself.

You do not know what you have. You are at the phase right now where you are still learning. I think that is the mistake of most prophets. They get over-confident and forget that they are still in a learning phase.

Do not be so arrogant as to think that you are the only one in the world that is right. Stop. If there is someone in your life that has always been spot on and hears the voice of the Lord, go to them and say, "What do you think?"

Then, have the humility and wisdom to hear what they have to say, whether it is in agreement with your revelation or not.

4. DO TEST THE SPIRIT

> *1 John 4:1 Beloved, do not believe every spirit, but test the spirits, whether they are of God; because many false prophets have gone out into the world.*

Test the spirit of any revelation that you get and any revelation that comes from someone else.

Anything that is forceful, pushy, produces guilt or fear, or anything that you are unsure of, test that spirit before taking action.

It does not mean that just because the word is negative that it is not of God. You cannot just throw the baby out with the bath water here. Some of the words that the prophets gave in the scriptures were not all, "You are blessed and will live happily ever after."

Some of their words were pretty tough. Jesus Himself said, "Jerusalem, you stoned the prophets. This temple will be torn down until not a stone is laid on top of another."

You can say, "That did not produce much faith, hope, or love."

However, the truth of Christ remained and from that was born the Early Church – the temple built by man was torn down, but the temple of the Holy Spirit was built from those ashes!

So, not every word has to be positive, but the spirit of it has to be true and pure. The Lord cried over Jerusalem and interceded over it.

Watch the spirit of any word.

5. DO NOT TALK TO ANGELS

Angels and demons are exciting subjects. I have already told you how to deal with demons.

Angels are messengers, servants. In the spirit, I see angels coming to bring scrolls in the spirit to indicate that God wants to give me a message. There are incidents in the Scriptures where angels appeared in actual bodily form and spoke to the people, but nobody sought angels out to have a conversation for the fun of it. Why do that when we can go to the Lord Himself?

Why mess around with the help, when you can sit down at the table and converse with the Master? Jesus is by far more interesting than any angel. Do not insult Him by seeking them out instead of His presence.

And so do not seek angels out or speak to them. We pray to the Lord, not angels!

KEY PRINCIPLE

> Do not seek to talk to angels.
> Instead, seek the presence of Jesus.

The minute you start seeking out angels, you end up like the Galatian church where they started worshipping angels. You will end up being keener to hear the voice of an angel than the voice of the Holy Spirit.

It is true, there are many in the Old Testament who heard God's instruction through the voice of angels, but let's fast forward to the New Testament.

In Acts 10 when Peter was on top of the house praying and the food came down, who spoke to him? Was it an angel? No, the Lord spoke to Him.

When Paul was struck to the ground and a voice spoke to him, who was it? Was it an angel? No, the voice said, "I am Jesus, who you are persecuting." Jesus spoke.

In every revelation that Paul shared, you will see that he said, "And the Lord said to me" not "And an angel said to me".

In the Old Testament, they did not have the indwelling of the Holy Spirit. So do not use that as your basis. They did not have righteousness in Christ. They had to come pure before the Lord, and they were not always so pure.

God could not remain with them. In the New Testament however, we have so much more. We do not have to go around speaking to angels. Why speak to the servant when you can speak to the headman, the boss?

Why would God send an angel to talk to you when you can hear from Him directly? I will tell you why some people hanker after it.

It is because it sounds so incredible to say, "I spoke to Gabriel the other day. He and I are buddies."

"Wow! Such a man of God. He speaks to angels."

The Word says that the angels are our servants. It does not say that they are our buddies and that we sit and talk to them. No angel died for me and saved me.

We have one Savior and if you want to get to the Father, it is through Jesus Christ and not through an angel. The angels do our bidding and they obey the

Word of God and they cause things to come to pass in the earth, according to the Word of God.

Yet, they are not there to have conversations with. If you are starting to talk to angels, you are getting sidetracked.

6. No Revelation on Demand

"I need a prophetic word."

Do you know how often we get that on a daily basis? One of our ministry team members will pick up the phone answering, "Apostolic Movement International" and the person on the other side will say, "Prophetic word, please."

I kid you not. The baffled response from the minister, "Excuse me?"

"Are you not a prophet in office?"

"Yes."

"So then, give me a prophetic word."

The obvious arrogance aside, it is the incorrect teaching on the prophetic ministry that has made this mess. They are taught that if you are a prophet, you are like a slot machine.

You put in the coin, pull the arm, and a prophetic word comes out.

If you allow yourself to be caught in that trap, stuff will come out, but whether or not what you are saying is really the word of God, you will never know.

A strong ministry standard that we cling to hinges off this point. We never give a prophetic word on demand. We will gladly pray on your behalf, minister, and even counsel you by the Word, but we will not ramble off the first thing that comes to our minds!

We speak as God tells us to speak, and that is that.

Remember the scripture I shared with you in 2 Peter 1 that says, "No man prophesied by his own will, but it was the Holy Spirit that gave the revelation?"

No man, through his own will, received prophecy. This is God's order of things. His gift – His rulebook!

We do not "work up" a prophecy. We do not say, "I want to get one so therefore I shall get one."

By all means, you can make yourself available and you can say, "Lord, this person needs you."

In such cases, we often say, "We will not give you a prophetic word, but if you have a need, we are more than happy to stand with you in prayer. Let's stand in agreement that the Lord will do something."

Who knows? Maybe the Lord will end up giving a revelation, but that is not for us to say. We can only be willing vessels. Do not go knocking down the gates of Heaven saying, "Give me a word."

Do not pick up the line to your Heavenly Father and say, "Prophetic word, please." Do not do it because it is against the Word of God and you are begging to get into deception.

7. Do Not Seek out the Sins of Others

"Father, please can you give me revelation on where my pastor is right now? Please give me revelation on what the sin is in his life. Please give me revelation on what is going on in this church."

None of this has anything to do with you! His sin is his sin and his problem is his problem. Do not put your nose into other people's business and ask God to give you revelation.

"Lord, please give me revelation what my husband's problem is. Please tell me what he is doing right now."

We have the Word of God for problems like this! If you ever want to see change in those around you, get a mirror because it starts in the face of your reflection.

"Lord, give me revelation why my son is in rebellion and my daughter is losing her conviction."

God will not reveal other people's sins to you. He will not give revelation about other people's sins, unless they are ready to repent. He is not going to say, "This person was browsing a site he should not and your daughter went to a friends house she should not have."

No, that is a spirit of divination, not the voice of the Lord!

He is not going to give you that kind of revelation unless it affects the work of God. Only then will God expose it.

However, He will expose it in His way and in His time. Do not go asking for revelation for things that do not concern you.

You are begging for deception. If you have done that, repent, deal with it and move on.

8. Deal With Preconceived Ideas.

This is a process and I cannot just leave this as a single point. Deal with your preconceived ideas. These are going to come from incorrect doctrines.

These are things that you always believed that preachers have preached from the pulpit again and again. Unfortunately, those teachings have become such a foundation in your life that they will even counteract the revelation that God is trying to give you.

As you have been going through this process, I have been using a lot of Scripture because I am trying to challenge your foundation.

Remember when I shared about having idols in your house and using those to reach God? That is a doctrinal problem. You have been taught that this is a good thing. It brings blessing and you can get into the anointing using it.

It is a doctrine and it is false. It has led you astray. Even when God tries to give you revelation, this doctrine stands in the way of you being able to hear God clearly.

If God has been challenging your doctrine and the things that you believe, then good! He is helping make sure that you do not have to walk in deception.

9. ASK FOR CONFIRMATION

I love having married couples work as ministry teams. Craig and I always work that way and I thank the Lord for it. I am in apostolic office, but I am not so arrogant that when I minister that I do not wait for confirmation from my husband.

We flow as a team. I will see that the Lord wants to release someone into apostolic training and I will say, "Ok Lord, I am waiting."

Then, Craig always has a revelation or gets a word that will be right in line with what God wants to do. Then I can stand up and release, impart and do what I need to do.

We take turns to share and God gives confirmation. It is a really solid backing. It is fantastic if you can minister with someone who is solid in the Word and Spirit.

Wait for that confirmation. People have this idea that if they do not share their revelation right now, all will be lost. It is not so. Wait. If the Holy Spirit comes back and nudges you say, "This is what I see and feel."

However, if you are ministering with a spouse or someone else, wait and give them a chance to share. The Lord will use them to confirm exactly what you sense.

There have been many times that I sense that the Lord wants to deal with something in someone's life, and I am not quite sure if I should engage just yet. The moment does not feel right, so I wait.

Then, suddenly they will say something and open it up wide. I will say, "That is exactly what I was sensing right now" and then I can jump right in.

APPLY THESE STEPS

If you can apply these steps, you are going to get through this phase with less scratches and bruises, and it will go a bit more smoothly.

In fact, you will survive it better than most.

It is not easy, but all is not lost if you miss it. That is why you are in a training phase. If you are learning to listen and practice your call in a safe environment, all is not lost.

Well, you could lose a bit of your pride, but other than that, the body of Christ will still remain from generation to generation. His believers are still in the palm of His hand.

You are not going to bring down the entire Christian church with your one, little deception. It is ok if you messed up. Recognize it, deal with it, and get back on track again.

Do you know what the most humbling part of all this is? God knew that you were going to get into deception, fail Him, and fall flat on your face. Yet, even before you took that wrong turn, He was preparing the way ahead of you to help you get back on your feet again.

It is not an easy process, but you can overcome, do it correctly, and rise up from this place.

One thing is for certain. When you have walked through this road, and you get to the other side, you will not feel like the big, conquering hero. You will stand in humility instead.

When someone dares to call you a prophet, you realize that you are not worthy to wear that title, or to have that authority because you know the weakness of your heart and the flaws of your flesh.

If this phase of prophetic deception accomplishes nothing more but that, then it has done its job.

What do you know prophet? You are closer to prophetic office than you realize.

I know that a prophetic trainee is ready when I get a message from them that says, "I do not know if I have what it takes. I always wanted to do this prophetic thing, but I do not think that I am ever going to get there. I do not think that I will ever be ready to be a prophet in office."

I get excited when that day comes, because I see something that they do not. I see the King raising His sword to knight them and set them in place. Not because they are worthy or more skillful than most. I know He has chosen them because they are completely His.

THE BEGINNING AND END OF WARFARE

CHAPTER 08 – THE BEGINNING AND END OF WARFARE

Only when you have gone through that crushing phase of prophetic training do you finally understand these two scriptures below.

These two scriptures should mean a lot to you right now if you have gone through the phase of prophetic deception and warfare that we have been talking about.

> *1 Corinthians 2:3 I was with you in weakness, in fear, and in much trembling.*

That is the thing with us overconfident prophets. When you first get the call, you are "gung ho." You say, "If you have a problem, I am there. If you need a prophetic word, I have it. If you need a demon cast out, I am your deliverance guy."

Then, after you hit your head a few times, you identify with the part that says "in fear and much trembling."

When someone asks you for a word again, you say, "I guess we can pray. Lord, please give me something. Anything. I hope I get revelation. I hope I am not missing it."

> *Philippians 2:12 Therefore, my beloved, as you have always obeyed, not as in my presence only, but now much more in my absence, work out your own salvation with fear and trembling.*

Apostle Paul knew how to keep us in line. He knew how to keep us on the road of humility.

We have been talking about how fear is negative, but this is not the type of fear that he is talking about here. I am not talking about a fear that is "unto death."

It is not a fear that makes you stop dead in your tracks. It is a cautious fear, a respect. It is a deep respect of the Holy Spirit, the realm of the spirit, and for the people that you are ministering to.

The prophet all on fire about being able to prophesy has lost his flamboyancy and has been replaced by a warrior with a hand securely on his sword, with eyes focused towards the goal.

You do not run headlong into battle just for the fun of it. Rather you stand silently on the battlefield saying, "Lord, I am available and I want you to use me, but if you do not show up, my weapons will be powerless."

THE HIDDEN SECRET

You have just engaged in the most defining phase of your training. A phase that not every prophet makes it through. Although I have given you a lot to learn and apply, you will still find yourself shaken up by the deception training phase.

You will find yourself unsure about every revelation you get. It will take you a little time to get the hang of knowing which voice is what. At first, you will wonder if anything you heard was from the Lord.

When you are at this point, then know this – you are about to discover the hidden secret of all true prophetic warriors.

> **KEY PRINCIPLE**
>
> This ministry is about His work. This is not about your call, your failure or your mistakes. This is about His kingdom.

You never started this journey to look good or walk in perfection. You did so to bless God's people. That is why you cannot go wrong with walking in love.

Sure, some of the words that you get may not be spot on. Some of the revelations that you receive may come straight out of your mind. Allow me the liberty to steal a page out of Apostle Paul's book and to tell you today, "Come... let me show you a better way."

> *1 Corinthians 13:1 Though I speak with the tongues of men and of angels, but have not love, I have become sounding brass or a clanging cymbal.*
> *2 And though I have the gift of prophecy, and understand all mysteries and all knowledge, and though I have all faith, so that I could remove*

mountains, but have not love, I am nothing.
3 And though I bestow all my goods to feed the
poor, and though I give my body to be burned,
but have not love, it profits me nothing.
4 Love suffers long and is kind; love does not
envy; love does not parade itself, is not puffed
up;
5 does not behave rudely, does not seek its own,
is not provoked, thinks no evil;
6 does not rejoice in iniquity, but rejoices in the
truth;
7 bears all things, believes all things, hopes all
things, endures all things.
8 Love never fails. But whether there are
prophecies, they will fail; whether there are
tongues, they will cease; whether there is
knowledge, it will vanish away. 9 For we know
in part and we prophesy in part.

When you can look through your mistakes, blood, sweat and tears to see your purpose, you will find that a single light shines through it all. It is when you have remained on the cross and allowed Jesus to get off. When you have fended off the hordes of hell in the lives of God's people.

When you have let go of your ideas and desires. When you have put everything you are on the altar, there will be just one thing that remains through it all.

Love.

Is this not the very thing that drew you to the call? Is it not the love of Jesus that has held you there through every fire? No matter how much you have failed, His love has continued to be a beacon of light in the darkness.

Every time you wanted to give up, His love compelled you forward. Every time you wanted to turn your back on Him, His love wooed you back. Each time you had no strength to carry on, His love put the sword back in your hand.

Don't you see it prophet of God? When you dissect your calling, training and all these principles, you find the single principle on which all the others are built.

Though you speak in tongues, prophesy or give up everything, it is the love with which you do these things that personifies your call. Which is better then? An accurate word given in arrogance, or a word of advice given in love?

Which do you think will have the greater impact on the heart of a blood-bought heir? If your motivation is love, advice can be transformed to revelation, and from there, released under the anointing.

Without love, your grand revelation is noisy in God's ears. When the love you have is for yourself instead of the Church, your prophesies are a "dripping tap" in the ears of God.

DROP THE PRINCIPLES

We get so hung up on principles and on whether or not it is the right time to speak.

"Is this voice of the Lord or not?"

"What demon am I coming against right now?"

"Is this a Urim or Thummim?"

"Is this a general or personal prophecy?"

There is a very big difference between principles and power!

KEY PRINCIPLE

> Principles will shape your mind, but it takes the power of God to change a heart.

As you have studied all of the books in this series, you have allowed them to shape the way you think. You have educated your mind and allowed the knowledge to become a foundation.

In the Old Testament we saw a God that gave us many gifts. The gift of life and the beauty of this world. In the New Testament though, we see a God who showed us His love – not just in the gifts He gave us – but in the life He laid down for us.

He cut past every law and statute of man. He completed every rule and met every expectation. He did it all with one force – the force of love.

Love lies at the core of your mandate as a prophet and as you prepare yourself for prophetic office, make sure that it is the foundation on which you stand.

THE "LOVE" RACK

The Pharisees came to Jesus and said, "What is the most important commandment?"

Jesus said in Matthew 22:37, *"That you love the Lord your God with all your heart, soul and mind and that you love your neighbor as yourself. On these hang all the law and the demands of the prophets."*

Then, He said to His disciples,

> *John 15:12 This is My commandment, that you love one another as I have loved you.*

Imagine a coat rack that everything else is positioned on. This pillar is, "Love one another as I have loved you."

That should be your motivation, the center of who and what you are. Love should dictate, when to speak and how to speak. Love should be the driving force behind whether or not you deal with a demon and all the other dos and don'ts that I have shared.

All the principles listed in every book in this series have a place on that rack and they are all motivated from this one pillar - love.

You can never go wrong with showing love and an act of compassion.

When the lepers and the blind man came to Jesus, the Word says that He was moved with compassion. He reached out with love.

He was hanging out with His disciples on the Sabbath and saw a woman that was bent over for many years. He was moved with love and compassion. Did He sit there with a list of principles?

KNOW LOVE AND COMPASSION

He did not stop to think. He simply reached out and healed her out of love and compassion.

What God has been trying to deal with you on is not what kind of demon you have.

What He has been doing is to bringing you to ponder, "What kind of love is motivating me?"

If that love did not originate from the Spirit, then it originated from the flesh. Do not think that just because you feel sorry for people that this pity, is love.

> ***KEY PRINCIPLE***
>
> What kind of love is motivating you?
> Love that originates from the Spirit
> has no rule, principle, or law that
> can stand against it.

No, that is just you imposing yourself and pushing your own agenda. However, love that originates from the Spirit, has no rule, principle or law that can stand against it.

It is a powerful force that should always motivate you. Yes, it is good to fill your mind with the knowledge that I have given you. It is good for you to remember these things, to memorize and know them, but love is always the key that turns the lock.

THE PRINCIPAL PRINCIPLE

If you can simplify everything you have learned so far into to one principle, this is it.

Your love should be greater than your fear of rejection.

Your love for others should be greater than your fear of getting into deception.

Your love should be greater than your fear of making a mistake.

Your love should be greater than your need to be noticed and affirmed.

God gives you a word and you begin wrapping off all the principles you have learned. You wonder if you should speak and if the person really needs to hear the word.

You are sitting in a meeting and someone is speaking heresy, leading the rest of the group astray. You think to yourself, "Well I do not want to impose my ministry. I know this is wrong, but I want to make sure I am saying this right."

It sounds very moral, but where does your love lie here? In your fear of rejection, or do you love these people enough to even get into trouble for them?

Sure it's not a bad idea to get wisdom before blurting out what you think, but there is nothing wrong with just stepping out and loving people. If you want an opportunity to minister, just start with the simplicity of love.

Love is greater than all your mistakes or successes. Love turns your focus off you "becoming a prophet" and turns it towards what God wants to do for His bride.

Your desire to flow in the gifts is left behind as you allow yourself to get swept away with wondering what God wants to do for that person in need.

Do you feel the shift? A change takes place at this phase from trying to seek the truth for your call and outwards to the role others play in God's plan.

Maturity is beginning to blossom in you and the banner spread over you is... love!

PRINCIPLES TO INSTINCT

The truth is, when you reach out to minister, you do not have time to think and apply the right principle.

When I was learning to play the drums, the Lord had to correct me because we would come into His presence, and I would be trying to practice instead of just worshipping Him.

I would be trying to learn how to get the drum roll or beat right, and it chased away the Holy Spirit. I sent the Dove flying out the window.

I learned that there was a time to practice and then a time to forget about if I was playing right and just let it go and worship the Lord!

I needed a balance of both. So, I would take times alone to practice and learn those drum rolls, patterns and beats that I wanted to learn. Then, when it came to flowing in the spirit in praise and worship, I forgot about all that technical stuff.

When I was worshipping the Lord, I did not stop and think, "I must hit this cymbal here or follow that beat there." I just did what was in me to do. The amazing thing is that I came to know what it meant to have the Holy Spirit take over!

Without even trying, I found the rolls and beats just bubbling out of me. The Holy Spirit took what I had programmed into my spirit during the practice sessions and used them in the praise sessions.

Now because my mind was not in the way, He could anoint my music and have me play any way that He wanted me to!

It is the same in your prophetic walk. There is a time to study and to show yourself approved. There is a time to learn the principles and digest the Word until it shapes you and becomes all you know.

When you step onto the battlefield though, it is not time to wonder whether to pick up your sword or put a stone in your sling. That should be instinctive. You should look down and see the sword in your hand, wondering how it got there. Principles become instinct and your walk becomes a process of doing God's will.

YOUR FINAL BATTLEFIELD

You do not realize how much you have changed or how much you have received. All these principles are swirling in your head like a soldier who has yet to face his first battle.

He expects the battlefield to be loud and the instructions of the Sergeant Major are still ringing in his ears. However, the moment he steps onto that field, everything will change.

All the principles will become silent and he will do what has become instinct. He will not remember the drills and the repetition of the principles. He will do naturally, what he was trained to do.

This is what I have been leading you up to. I have drilled you, challenged you and repeated the same things over and over again.

You cannot bear to hear me say one more time, "The core of every revelation should always be faith, hope and love."

If I have to tell you one more time that a prophet should be leading the church into a face-to-face relationship with Jesus, you are ready to throw the book at me!

You know that fear is of the devil and the Lord leads, He does not push from behind. Tell me prophet, why do you know these things? It is because you have trained your mind with them.

Now when you stand in your next battle, you will put all that aside. You will be like Jesus who was led into the wilderness to face his final test before rising up and beginning His ministry.

After years of training in obscurity, the Son of Man is lead into the wilderness and the devil comes and engages Him in warfare. With each temptation though, the Word rose up out of Jesus. The years of learning and sticking close to the Father enabled Him to pass the tests.

These same convictions were the foundation that he left behind three years later. When you are standing toe to toe with the enemy, these principles will seem to have vanished into the air.

What would have remained though would be what was imparted to you. The convictions you received. The truth that you have clung to. The vessel you have become through the shaping of the Holy Spirit is what will remain.

In this moment you will not need my voice to remind you who you are in Christ. A mighty warrior will break out of deep within you and you will look the devil in the eye and also say to him, "Get you behind me satan!"

All you have learned and all the training you have gone through will not be a list of principles. They will be the living Word. A word transformed into power.

> *Luke 4:14 Then Jesus returned in the power of the Spirit to Galilee, and news of Him went out through all the surrounding region.*

I, Colette Toach, cannot make you into a prophet. No man on earth can do that. I cannot give you any power or anointing, only the Holy Spirit can do that!

Jesus was alone when He faced the devil, and after that encounter, this passage tells us that he returned full of dynamic power to do the work.

It is indeed dark when you are led down to the valley of the shadow of death. The darkness seems to press in on you. However, when you overcome that test and wax strong in spirit, you will discover dynamic power!

THE BEGINNING AND THE END OF PROPHETIC WARFARE

This is why we go to war. We go to war to take the land because we love God's people. When that is your motivation, love is the beginning and the end of warfare.

Why do you labor long with someone who is demonized? It is because you know that love is the only healer.

Love is the one thing that the enemy cannot comprehend. It is light, and he cannot comprehend this light.

When you take that motivation of love, the authority, the principles, the Word of God and everything else, it is obvious what to do.

When you look at a person and your heart is moved with compassion, it is obvious what to do.

Jesus gave up His very life so that we can have this authority to bind every demon in Hell.

His love was the beginning and end of our warfare two thousand years ago and all we need to do now is stand on His victory.

Love is the beginning and the end of warfare.

You do not have to run around looking for warfare. Stay where you are. It will come to you soon enough.

Warfare will be found through the lives that you reach and the people that you meet. It will find you as you "build up" and "tear down." It will come at you during your times of intercession.

When it does, you will know what to do. You can rest now, knowing that you are both armed and ready.

> *1 Corinthians 13:13 And now abide faith, hope, love, these three; but the greatest of these is love.*

ABOUT THE AUTHOR

Born in Bulawayo, Zimbabwe and raised in South Africa, Colette had a zeal to serve the Lord from a young age. Coming from a long line of Christian leaders and having grown up as a pastor's kid she is no stranger to the realities of ministry. Despite having to endure many hardships such as her parent's divorce, rejection, and poverty, she continues to follow after the Lord passionately. Overcoming these obstacles early in her life has built a foundation of compassion and desire to help others gain victory in their lives.

Since then, the Lord has led Colette, with her husband Craig Toach, to establish *Apostolic Movement International,* a ministry to train and minister to Christian leaders all over the world, where they share all the wisdom that the Lord has given them through each and every time they chose to walk through the refining fire in their personal lives, as well as in ministry.

In addition, Colette is a fantastic cook, an amazing mom to not only her 4 natural children, but to her numerous spiritual children all over the world. Colette is also a renowned author, mentor, trainer and a woman that has great taste in shoes! The scripture to "be all things to all men" definitely applies here, and the Lord keeps adding to that list of things each and every day.

How does she do it all? Experience through every book and teaching the life of an apostle firsthand, and get the insight into how the call of God can make every aspect of your life an incredible adventure.

Read more at www.colette-toach.com

Connect with Colette Toach on Facebook!
www.facebook.com/ColetteToach

Check Colette out on Amazon.com at:
www.amazon.com/author/colettetoach

RECOMMENDATIONS BY THE AUTHOR

Note: All reference of AMI refers to Apostolic Movement International.

If you enjoyed this book, we know you will also love the following books on the prophetic.

PROPHETIC ESSENTIALS

Book 1 of the Prophetic Field Guide Series

By Colette Toach

In this book, you will find out that the call of the prophet goes far deeper than the functions and duties that the prophet fulfills. Anyone flowing in prophetic ministry can carry out tasks similar to the prophet.

If it burns in you to pay any price that is necessary and to stand up and break down the barriers between the Lord Jesus and His Bride, then my friend, you have picked up the right tool that will confirm the fire in your belly and the call of God on your life.

If you go through the pages of this book, you will no longer see prophecy and prophetic ministry as the beginning and end of the prophetic call. You will cross a threshold and be thrust into the fullness of the call and responsibility of God's true prophet.

PROPHETIC FUNCTIONS

Book 2 of the Prophetic Field Guide Series

By Colette Toach

There is so much more to the prophet than standing up in church and prophesying.

Laid out beautifully so that you can understand and relate, Colette Toach shares from her own personal experiences. She uses both the Word and the Spirit - a rare combination, to drive the point home. Be prepared to live and experience the Lord like never before. This is not fiction... this is your training guide to the prophetic.

PROPHETIC ANOINTING

Book 3 of the Prophetic Field Guide Series

By Colette Toach

God has promised you a visit to the throne room! This is your summons from Almighty God. It is time for you to experience Him face-to-face and heart-to-heart.

Get ready for the meeting of a lifetime. The veils that have hindered the anointing in your life are going to be ripped away, and you are going to shine with His glory in every area of your life.

PROPHETIC BOOT CAMP

Book 4 of the Prophetic Field Guide Series

By Colette Toach

The way of the prophet is one that goes through the cross, surrenders in death and rises up in resurrection power and authority. Deep inside you know that you have not gone through this hard road just to come out defeated. You have paved the way for others.

So, prophet of God, are you ready to sign up for boot camp?

PROPHETIC WARFARE

Book 5 of the Prophetic Field Guide Series

By Colette Toach

A true warrior holds no excuses of why he cannot defeat his enemy and so is true with a genuine prophet of God. He is ready to take up the weapons of warfare that God has prepared for Him and to set the captive free and to heal the broken hearted.

Prophet of God, now is the time to face your own limitations and your own bondages and to see what has been holding you back from walking as the warrior that God has called you to be.

A.M.I. Prophetic School

www.prophetic-school.com

 Whether you are just starting out or have been along the way for some time, we all have questions.

Who better to answer them than another prophet!

With over 18 years of experience, the A.M.I. Prophetic School is the leader in the prophetic realm.

From dedicated lecturers to live streaming and graduation, the A.M.I. Prophetic School is your home away from home.

What Our Prophetic Training Accomplishes

Our extensive training is a full two-year curriculum that will:

1. Identify and confirm your prophetic call
2. Effectively train you to flow in all the gifts of the Spirit
3. Fulfill your purpose as a prophet in the local church
4. Take your hand through the prophetic training process
5. Specialist training in spiritual warfare
6. Arm you for intercession and decree
7. Minister in praise and worship
8. Achieve prophetic maturity

CONTACT INFORMATION

To check out our wide selection of materials, go to:
www.ami-bookshop.com

Do you have any questions about any products?

Contact us at: +1 (760) 466 - 7679
(8am to 5pm California Time, Weekdays Only)

E-mail Address: admin@ami-bookshop.com

Postal Address:

> A.M.I.
> 5663 Balboa Ave #416
> San Diego, CA 92111, USA

Facebook Page:
http://www.facebook.com/ApostolicMovementInternational

YouTube Page:
https://www.youtube.com/c/ApostolicMovementInternational

Twitter Page: https://twitter.com/apmoveint

Amazon.com Page: www.amazon.com/author/colettetoach

AMI Bookshop – It's not Just Knowledge, It's **Living Knowledge**

Made in the USA
Columbia, SC
27 March 2020

89970393R10120